Buddhas in Disguise

Irene Taylor

Buddhas in Disguise

Deaf People of Nepal

DawnSignPress

San Diego, California

Producer: Joe Dannis
Designer: Michel H. Makhoul
Printed in Hong Kong by Global Interprint
Published by DAWNSIGNPRESS

Library of Congress Cataloging-in-Publication Data
Taylor, Irene.
        Buddhas in disguise : deaf people of Nepal / Irene Taylor.
                p.   cm.
        ISBN 0-915035-59-6 (alk. paper)
        1. Deaf–Nepal–Social conditions.. 2. Nepal–Description and travel.
        I. Title.
        HV2855.9.T39 1997
        305.9'08162'095496–dc21   97-791
                                                                            CIP

10   9   8   7   6   5   4   3   2   1

To my Mother and Father,
for showing me how to live within two worlds.

Buddhist musical instruments, hats, and horns

Contents

A Buddhist pilgrim reaches his head toward a doorway to the gods at Muktinath, a sacred destination for travelers of varying faiths. Above the entrance to the Hindu temple are pictures of the king of Nepal and his wife. The king is believed to be an incarnation of the all-preserving Lord Vishnu.

Acknowledgments

I am grateful to the many who have helped in creating this book.

My work has brought countless wonderful beings into my life. I am filled with gratitude for the wonder and grace the people of Nepal and Tibet have given to me. This book is for them, and yet too many of them will never know that it has come to pass. For those unwitting teachers and subjects whom I met perhaps on a trailside, inside a tea shop, or while crossing a mountain pass together sharing one another's pack loads, I am especially thankful.

I could not possibly have photographed so energetically without the help of those jovial and hard-working guides and porters who trekked the trail in front of me, alongside me and, sometimes, behind me, carrying our tents and rice. Special thanks go to Karma Rapkye Lama of Dolpo, who through his wonderful guidance across some forbidding lands brought me onto the paths of countless countrymen and women, whose teapots overflowed and whose homes were open to me for both work and friendship.

The Nepalese of Lumbini, Helambu, Dolpo, Mustang and Upper Ghorka all dutifully gave of what little time they had left after a day's work.

For their patient explanations of religious traditions across Nepal and for their generous hospitality, I remember fondly the lamas of Serang Gompa and my long-standing friendship with "Baba" Devi Prasad Paudel of Lumbini.

I would also like to pay tribute to the critical work now being done in Nepal by ear, nose and throat surgeon Dr. Yanta Mani Pradhan and his Nepali Operation Eyesight team. Traveling to medical camps across some of the most remote areas of Nepal, they were always ready to give me a seat in their truck, Twin Otter plane, or even—where the trail was especially rough—on horseback on a colorful Tibetan saddle. For the many Nepalis they put in my pathway, and their patience with my camera and my endless questions, I am especially thankful.

The Deaf associations of Kathmandu, Lumbini, and the Gandaki Zone were all instrumental in the creation of my ideas and projects here in Nepal. Some workers in these associations are silent soldiers, others are rowdy mavericks of an emerging Deaf culture in Nepal; their *Ishara* sign ballads have been an inspiration to all of us who have worked with them.

Sincerest gratitude must also be paid to my language teachers, Ghokal Risal, Sushila Bhuju, and Tinley Lama, for giving me the tools to communicate in Nepali Sign Language, Nepali and Tibetan, respectively. Their guidance and friendship has allowed me to tap into so much across the country.

Besides the many who have inspired this work, I am thankful to those who helped produce the book itself. Back in the United States, I send appreciation to Tom Raco, Antonio Toscano, Michael Spencer, and Dr. Bill Castle and the faculty of the Photo/Media Department of the National Technical Institute for the Deaf in Rochester, New York, for their generous offerings of their state-of-the-art darkroom facilities and technical advice. Their professional mentorship, personal encouragement, and faith in my work laid the groundwork for the road upon which I have traveled over the last two years in developing this book.

Further, I am grateful to those who put my words to their test. For sharing their insights on the first drafts of the manuscript, I wish to thank Lou Ann Walker, Frances M. Parsons and

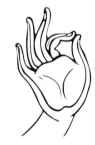

2

Bathing on the shores of the Bagmati river in Kathmandu cleanses pilgrims of their karma. According to Hindus, ritual cleansing is an important contribution towards their physical well-being.

Dr. T. Alan Hurwitz, for their Deaf perspectives, Vidhea Shrestha, Phuntsog Dhakpotsang, and Tirtha Lama of Kathmandu, for their diligent review of my Nepali phrases and cultural notes. Sonia Jaffe-Robbins and Tom Schlegel extended their keen Editor's hands with a balance of discipline, encouragement, and craft. Thanks to Tom especially for greet-ing my ideas with the inquisitiveness of a teacher, and the grace of a friend. He certainly intercepted an overwhelmed traveler and helped to bring the book back home again, to where it all began.

For his open-mindedness and generosi-ty, thanks go to my publisher, Joe Dannis. He has been a faithful pen pal and cer-tainly a thought-provoking advocate of Deaf culture around the world.

On a more personal note, I extend loving thanks to my family for their book-keeping, faithful faxing, generosity of their cameras and, especially, patience for all the holidays I've missed back home. By no means have they been silent bystanders on this journey.

To my Nepali family, Larkyl, Karmu, Kusang and Dawa Lama, I love your gentle hearts. Thank you for the many silent teachings you have offered over our never-ending bowls of butter tea and beef thukpa in your mountain land of Helambu.

I am continually indebted to the Deaf people I meet in both the East and the West. For those of us fortunate enough to see beyond your silent disguise, what visual landscapes we have learned to travel! Thank you!

Preface

Be not forgetful to entertain strangers:

For thereby some have entertained angels unawares.

Hebrews 13:2

Once there was a lone traveler making his perilous way across the expansive plateau of Tibet. Exhausted and without food, he was in immediate danger of losing his life when he came upon a young girl tending a herd of yaks. She took the weary man into her tent, nursed him back to health, and fed him until his strength returned. As the man was recovering, he observed the girl was alone and doing the work that even a number of strong men would have found difficult.

Eventually, he was fit to travel again and the girl sent him on his way with some provisions. Although it was a long journey, the man discovered that the food she had given him never ran out until he was back in his own valley. Marveling at all that had happened, he went to the village lama (priest) with his story, wondering if the young girl could secretly have been White Tara, known as the seven-eyed, all-seeing, female buddha to the people of the *Himalaya*. "Of course she was," the lama reprimanded him. "How could you not have recognized the kind and compassionate heart behind her disguise?"

Hindu Pilgrim bathing at the Bagmati river, Pashupatinath, Kathmandu.

Tara is known to be wandering throughout the *Himalaya* still today. Like many other buddhas who have already attained enlightenment, Tara still roams the Earth disguised as a simple, often needy, human being in order to be a teacher of compassion to all of mankind.

"That is why we say in Tibet that the beggar who is asking you for money, or the sick old woman wringing your heart, may be the buddhas in disguise, manifesting on your path to help you grow in compassion . . ." the living Tibetan master Sogyal Rinpoche has said. *"Compassion is a far greater and nobler thing than pity . . .'When your fear touches someone's pain, it becomes pity; when your love touches someone's pain, it becomes compassion.'"*[1]

Both urban and rural, deaf and hearing, Nepalese folk often ask me why I seek out Deaf people. Am I a doctor?

An aid worker?

A missionary?

My work is never as clear-cut as that, and so this has become a difficult and pressing question to answer, even for myself. I have had a lot of time to think about it, walking six, eight, sometimes twelve hours a day across Nepal; my boots no longer make a sound as they touch the earth with each meditative step. In retrospect, my answers have been everywhere. With a little magic and a lot of photography, I have begun to recognize the footprints of White Tara crisscrossing my pathway. In brothels of Kathmandu and smoky Himalayan kitchens, across snow-covered mountain passes and dirt roads ravaged by the monsoon rains, I find traces of the buddhas all around me. Hidden within the voiceless ones, latent in flying hands and foreboding gazes, are the teachers of the golden rules of the East. My job has been simply to watch, very closely, all that they have to say.

Setting Out

I got my first lesson in deafness, or at least, what I thought was deafness, when I was eight. My sister Lucy and I used to play games with sound. We would sit in the kitchen and listen to Mom's old Regulator clock to see how long it would take to actually recognize the tick-tock sound of its ever-swinging pendulum.

The Regulator was an antique that Mom bought shortly after I was born, hoping it would lull me to sleep each night. It was in the shape of a top-heavy figure eight carved in varnished wood with an impressive octagonal face on top. Pointing to the time were slender black hands, coming to the same spaded point that was a theme throughout my mother's kitchen. Below, in the smaller glass case, was the pendulum, counting seconds, a perfectly round brass piece that never sat still. The pendulum had predictability and precision. Its job was to capture time and play it for us.

I was deaf to its swing. I would stare that pendulum down incredulously, concentrating intently, my eyes swinging back and forth like windshield wipers as I tried to get the message to travel clearly from my ears into my brain. Sometimes it took as long as a full minute before I realized any sound.

The curious thing was, none of us could hear the Regulator. The tick-tock had embedded itself into the brain of my brother as well, so that for each of us the sound translated into the mundane footwork of a silent dancer. Thereby the pendulum mesmerized, it transformed; my childish wonder world became more the adult world of my parents. The thought of it absolutely thrilled me.

My mother and father are deaf. As for any young child growing up, they were my whole world. My standard. My center. My life has always been surrounded by deaf people. As a young girl, I spent school vacations skateboarding the underground tunnels of the National Technical Institute for the Deaf. I spent my teenage years living on the campus of a residential deaf school in England and my college days working as an interpreter to get through school. Some of my earliest memories are of Mom singing to me, her hands and mouth lullabying in unison to bring me her song. Dad, it seems, was forever creating something down in his workshop, the floors covered with old-fashioned teletype bodies and the confetti of ticker tape, his inventions all neatly bisected with saw horses, his shelves stocked with photographic chemicals. Together, my parents built us our first darkroom.

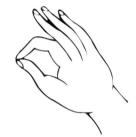

It was around the time my parents began mastering American Sign Language, in their late twenties, that they began to take a keen interest in photography. Much like the poetic lexicon of the language of sign, a photograph is succinct yet vague; it both embodies meaning and diffuses it. Perhaps because I never mastered sign language as naturally as my parents did, photography became my way of personalizing a similarly rich and visually symbolic language. For each of us, our new modes of communicating provided a direct and more visceral way to communicate with other people. Our communication required no interpreters, only the doorway of one's two eyes. The barriers so traditionally present between the Taylors and the world around us have since worn down into only a thin veil, one that protects the magic and mystery in a world of silence, one that protects the sanctity of the memories of a family.

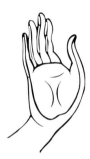

Nowadays, the spirit of that old Regulator pendulum lives on inside my Nikon viewfinder, transforming experience into my own silent soliloquy.

This is a book about deaf people and my relationship to them. They come from the many different backgrounds, castes, livelihoods and regions of the small Himalayan Kingdom of Nepal. They are tailors from small villages in Asia's Gangetic Basin plain, yak herders traveling through high mountain settlements, and prostitutes in Kathmandu's most ancient neighborhoods. Some are activists and community leaders living in the country's swelling urban centers. Most are confined to their own world, the ways of their ethnic clan or caste, and to the demands of their environment. Like most Nepalis, they reap their livelihoods tilling the land and cooperating with the gods.

I, on the other hand, come from the banks of the Mississippi, the bayous of east Texas, and the urban and suburban streets of New York. We are of two different worlds, and theirs is a more precarious existence. It is difficult to tell whether their lives manifest reality's magician or its master.

This is also a book about Nepal. There are many ways to look at Nepal, especially photographically. Go into any bookstore in Kathmandu or New York City and there are feasts of imagery from central Asia: the pervasive eyes of Buddha etched upon religious relics and colorful mountainside *stupas*, esoteric holy men wandering from city alleyways into the backbone of Himalayan valleys, undulating riverbeds pouring from the world's tallest mountain peaks, malnourished children smiling and poking fun at some camera lens. But the camera can distort, mislead and falsely inspire. Photographs can make swindlers look like wise men just as they can disembody the wealth of the human spirit.

I've tried to be honest, to introduce Nepal much in the same way I first came to it myself, through deaf people. Nepalis are as diverse as the languages they speak, the gods they honor, and the lay of their land; trying either to distinguish or to generalize about them is an impossible task indeed. By focusing on the experiences of deaf people, their families, and the scattered cultural pockets they live in, I have taken an unlikely approach to Nepal.

The entryway has been marked with both romance and disgust. To be deaf in Nepal is likened to a curse. On a social level, deaf people are considered to be on the lowest rungs, along with untouchables and other low-caste members. In this society where survival is a delicate balance of the wits of men and women, the land, and the unpredictable folly of both benevolent and wrathful deities, most deaf people are just getting their most basic needs met. Deaf people are ostracized. People commonly poke fun at them, throw stones at those who cannot speak, and talk behind the eyes of a deaf person as if he didn't exist. They have few opportunities to develop a language, much less get an education. Many deaf people I met did not know their own name, or even that people have names.

Coming from the Western world to Nepal for the first time, anything I once presumed to know about deafness slipped through the very fingers that had now gone mute and could no longer communicate with those deaf around me. My experiences seemed irrelevant, both my native signed and spoken languages obsolete. What I thought was right, or socially desirable, suddenly was wrong here. Traveling to the other side of the earth threw me behind a barrier into the same kind of territory that my parents have lived their whole lives. I was the outsider now. I couldn't communicate or relate to any of the subtleties going on around me. Following the Eastern path of death and rebirth, I had died and was reborn into this alien world. It was only after I had seen this basement of my existence that I could start over again. With camera in hand, I began my journey.

The beginning was not easy. Although I quickly picked up Nepali Sign Language and survival spoken Nepali, I would always be a *bideshi* (foreigner) and, moreover, a woman. Even further, among more educated deaf communities, I had yet a third strike against me: my hearing world. I was another white, wealthy, colonialist face.

Long before I ever arrived, the British had come to neighboring India. Although they never actually ruled Nepal, their 300-year stay next door left a bad taste in the mouth of some Nepalis, who even today resent and resist foreign influence and power. Deaf Nepalis are no excep-

tion. For years, their native signs were frowned upon, and the educated few were taught either British Sign Language or how to speak and lipread spoken tongue. Whether deaf or hearing, colonial culture taught Nepalis that their native languages and corresponding cultures were backward and primitive. Even today, using English of the Western world is a desirable standard, and there is relatively little appreciation for the articulation of either spoken or signed Nepali. For a deaf person to speak, or a Nepali to know English, is encouraged foremost as a sign of progress and intelligence.

When I arrived in Nepal with my Western nametag and only vague job descriptions, understandably some were suspicious of my willingness to "help." To others, my friendship was mistaken as an instant and direct path to a new job, a sponsored son or daughter, or social popularity. Either way, amongst the more organized deaf communities in the urban areas especially, it took some time to develop trust and common ground, not only between our contrasting cultures of Nepal and America, but even more so between our deaf and hearing worlds.

It is my sincere hope that this book will provide a bridge for understanding those contrasting worlds. Although many of the photographs in this book do not include deaf people, implicitly they concern them, because Nepal is their center and the root of their existence from which they are born and grow. For most, this culture is all they know. There is no plane ticket or running water waiting back at the hotel room. International development cannot change their lives or create opportunities overnight. Nor should it.

Without the options often available to those living in more developed countries, deaf Nepalis have little chance but to work inside of the prescribed Nepali life with people whose language and culture they most often do not understand. They join in prayer to gods who, in their mind's eye, have neither name nor meaning. Yet deaf and hearing routinely till land together, harvest crops together, and do their share of house chores for the benefit of the greater community; they survive together. In the most critical of mountain areas especially, I have seen little ground left for barriers.

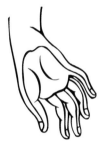

THE KINGDOM OF NEPAL

TIBET

INDIA

by Art:

When my mind recalls home, I am saddened by the divisions existing not just between hearing and deaf people, but between deaf and deaf people. It is ironic how the development of better medical care, social service, and legal access in the United States have now created ideological rifts among the Deaf community. Because deafness is no longer perceived as a public health "problem," deaf people are asserting a new identity for themselves. Many want an ethnic title within the diversity of our increasingly global communities. Others prefer a lower profile and resent being recruited into a cultural army in which they never enlisted. Either way, as they continue to struggle with a way to deal with their crusades, the realities of Nepal could drift further into the distance.

In trying to break down old barriers, new ones can be created. Very few Western deaf people, or those otherwise interested in deaf issues, see beyond the tips of their own fingers, which is a shame.

Nepal and Eastern thought has much to teach us in the West. To ponder Nepal we are required to step back from the sharply defined ideals that we revere in the West and inquisitively wander into the often mysterious, often chaotic, Eastern hinterlands. From their religious dharma to their daily routines, contemporary Nepali lives are testament to that vague wonder that sits warily between right and wrong and to that which is morally gray. There is no black and white for them; what may be one man's gospel may be another's lament.

It wasn't long after I arrived in Nepal that I could see my Western ideals could not fully apply to my work. Whereas I began a romantic journey into the heart of Nepal's traditions and landscape, I soon found conflict in where it was taking me. Within the integrity of an ancient and varied culture thrived age-old supersitions tormenting the lives of those born to a lesser God. Whether they be deaf or simply born into a low caste, the beautiful valleys that glorified the landscape could at the same time be a trench to those who were of a supposedly slighter breed, to those who were different. Just like the diverse pantheon of wrathful and benevolent gods sharing their mountain peaks, riverbeds, and temples, I came to realize that beauty and evil will sit side by side.

Nepal today is a land of such paradoxes, and there are no black and white approaches, no right or wrong ways, to approach her world of deaf people. What can I say of the families who have four, maybe five deaf children, all of whom have been deafened from disease thriving in a dirty water tap in their village? That we shouldn't try to prevent their next child from becoming deaf too? How can I tell parents practicing ancient family customs that their congenitally deaf son or daughter now belongs to another culture, the Deaf Culture, and that no medicine can bridge those two worlds? In villages two weeks from the nearest road head, I've given medicine out of my own first-aid kits that would combat acute cases of "glue ear" and perhaps prevent a full-blown case of deafness. Does this mean I am fighting, or am "against" deaf people when some Nepalis' deafness is literally killing them? After full days meeting with deaf children and seeing how their families have been entrenched into a cycle of poverty, I've lost my appetite and ran away into rice fields crying and cursing deafness in bewildered frustration. Does this mean deafness is a "tragedy"? The stories and photographs of this book attempt to answer such questions, but they also raise new ones that can invite readers to understand a world of Deaf people, and Nepal, in a new way.

Do not mistake my assessment of these people as pity. I have tried to tell their story as accurately as I know how, with the same compassion as those courageous few I have met in Nepal who are daring to step outside of their social sphere and travel a new road, one that is increasingly open to people of all varying abilities and ethnic groups. Further, do not dismiss my personal accounts as mere sentiment. Having been disenchanted and turned off by the dry, academic accounts of deafness in Nepal spoken of in medical and foreign aid circles, I have attempted to give a more subjective account that takes into account many of the more intimate moments between myself and the deaf people of Nepal. It is through these stories and their own words that I hope readers will discover the subtle rhythms of Nepali life and how these make the question of deafness so problematic.

Living between the Deaf and Hearing worlds, the Eastern and Western worlds, my own answers dangle, my boundaries constantly ebb and flow. If this book stirs readers, if it proposes questions that can't quite be answered, then I have completed my task. No answers will be permanent. I know now.

The buddhas showed me so.

Templescape Patan Durbar Square,
Kathmandu Valley.

Where Are the Buddhas?

Tibetan Buddhist Nyingmapa monks sound their ritual horns in the early morning.

A mother holds the hand of her only child as they make their way through the early morning winter fog beside the road climbing out of the valley of Kathmandu. She is wearing her best sari, red and glittery gold to match her glass bangles and the *tika* that sits just above and between her dark brown eyes. She has dressed her son in a traditional cotton *daura surwal*, long shirt and pants, a woolen vest, and black lace-up school shoes. It is by providence that the child was born of this place.

Together they make their way, as they have done ritually one Tuesday of each winter for the past four years, to the *Surya Binayak* temple, the "Sun Abode of the Shrew." The home of

12   *A monk walks the path to Serang Gompa, a temple belonging to Tibetan Buddhism's oldest school, the Nyingmapa sect. Serang is located in one of the Himalaya's remote "Hidden Valleys," symbolic havens of refuge for Buddhists in time of spiritual, social, or political strife.*

legendary Ganesh, the elephant god of wisdom, this pagoda temple sits high on a hill ten miles from Kathmandu. Hundreds come daily to appease the deities who are at play in the skies above them. Whether by folly or by their disciplined wisdom, the gods and goddesses will decree the fates of all those below and around them; they will hold back the rains, bring forth bounty, give and take away all that is life. The faithful walk miles approaching the steps of God's doorway, singing doxologies and chanting ritual prayers. With their brass offering vessels, they come to offer sweets and eggs, rice, small *rupee* notes and *paisa* coins. They burn incense and give *tikas* of crushed vermilion and marigolds to the monuments and statues that sit enthroned among the ancient templescape.

Seeking special favor today, the mother has dutifully packed a live, fattened, chicken that now flutters inside her young son's burlap bag. Together they climb the winding white-washed steps scattered with pigeons, blind and footless beggars, and ascetic men and women, to reach the pulpit of the temple deities. Spotting the head *Brahmin* priest, the mother respectfully calls upon him to lead them further into the jungle overhead and beyond. At the top of the hill, where the fog sits over their morning like a mother hen hovering over her hatch, the *Brahmin* takes the boy's hand, leading him away from the small concrete temple at the top of the hill. He brings him into a wooded sanctuary and leaves him there, where the child is instructed to sit among towering

A Hindu worshipper places flowers, rice and vermilion powder in reverence to the Lord Shiva, the Destroyer.

13

14 *A mountain child together with elder village girls. They often help care for small children while their parents work in the fields.*

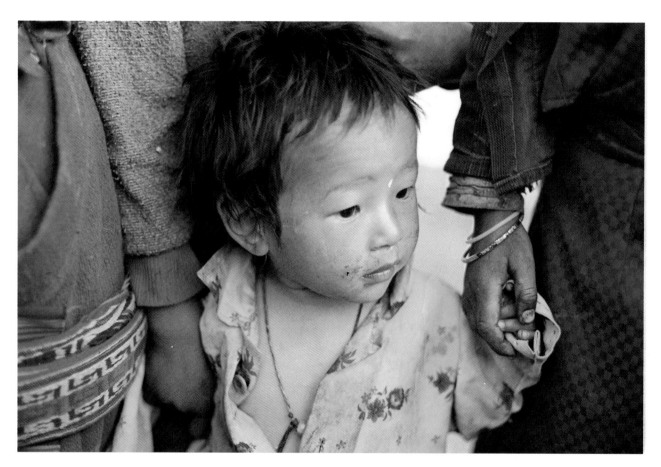

trees and the song of early morning birds he cannot hear.

The boy hasn't spoken a word in his five years. He has been brought to the temple in a last attempt to bring words from his mouth and sense to his spirit. Over the five years, to persuade the deities to redirect their aggression, his parents have done everything to placate

gods through daily ritual *puja* and the sacrificial offerings of several chickens and one goat.

Closely following the Hindu tradition, many children who cannot speak are brought each year and left to sit alone in this forest high above the *Surya Binayak*. The child is left alone all day and into the night, while the priest watches closely to

Monks and Lamas (graduated scholars of Buddhism) welcome the arrival of Dudrupchen Rinpoche, "greatly precious" and an especially qualified master of their faith in Mahayana Buddhism.

see if the fear of sitting alone in this foreboding place can bring words, even if just a scream or cry. Only the gods, the Nepali people believe, can restore that which has been taken away at birth. Only they can arbitrate the play of hostile forces of life and death circling in the elements of the Earth, the human body, and the soul. They are ultimately merciful, yet regularly wrathful. In the desperation of human existence, only such gods can prove their steadfastness.

So these rituals are performed to request the deities' benevolence and their mercy. After five annual efforts of visiting the *Surya Binayak*, if still no words come from the child's mouth then efforts cease. His fate becomes indelibly written

16 *Mahayana Buddhist Monks and Lamas.*

and accepted. The ritual dies and a new life is born: the life of a *latto*, the Nepali name given to the speechless, the silent ones, the "dumb." Neither the gods nor the priests will do anything more to interfere with such a fate.

In Nepal, upon discovering a person is without speech or the sense of hearing, there begins a calamitous attempt to

reverse what is considered a curse upon both the individual and his or her family. According to Nepali beliefs and understanding, the lack of speech has more to do with the play of the gods than with any medical diagnosis of hearing loss. It is only the local healer or priest, not a doctor or the sensitivity of another deaf person, that can confirm this aggression

of the spirits that is otherwise known as deafness. All over Nepal, people cry out to the same deity with a thousand different names, for mercy, to be spared from such a burden.

One day south, in the Gangetic plains near the Indian border, a Hindu *Brahmin* pundit (priest) tells his own story:

A deaf child in the remote Dolpa district of Nepal's Himalayan region. Sufficient clothing and hygiene are hard to come by in most mountain communities, and deaf children often receive sub-standard care.

Eighteen years ago a mother brought her eight-year-old child to me and left him. She said she would come back after one week, but she didn't come. ...Many months later the mother still had not come, so this was a problem for me... The child was deaf, his ears could not hear and his mouth could not speak, that was why his mother did not come to take him. I think the mother was trying to abandon him and skip out on her one responsibility...

...When they brought him to me they thought they could just deliver their son or daughter to me, as if to admit him so that I could do something for him. They thought they could just give me their burden. It was very hard for me to feed him and put him to sleep.

18   *Seven-years-old and deaf,*
      Lalita Gurung at home in
      central Nepal.

My language was not compatible with his, that is why it was so difficult to get to know him... Learning how to communicate with him was more difficult than the expense of keeping him ever was. ... After that, I understood how they felt. If they could just release that burden, they didn't mind how much they would have to pay.

Meanwhile, in a valley hamlet deep in the Buddhist hinterland of the *Himalaya* 100 miles north, a mother gives birth to a deaf son. Her family has no riches to offer the gods or their priestly messengers, but dutifully she will take her child to the local *jhankri* (shaman) to offer penance, just as she has done for her four other deaf sons

Deaf students outside one of Nepal's four government schools for deaf children.

born in the years before this one. She knows the ritual well.

Just as dutifully, the *jhankri* will dance around the child and beat his drum while entering into a trance. His job is to invoke and internalize the evil spirit afflicting the child, digest its wrath, and then dispose of it where it belongs, back into the dark spirit world. The *jhankri* and the parents know just what to do, playing a game with the gods that they sense already they have lost. One in four of their village children become deaf and, compared with the shadow of death that comes so easily knocking at their doors, this hearing loss is accepted as the wrath of a lesser, more benevolent God.

Phoksumdo Lake, known in Nepali as "Ringmo," marks the entryway into the Tibetan-speaking region of inner Dolpo. One of Nepal's largest high-altitude lakes, it rests at 11,700 feet and stretches three miles long.

The Divine Canvas

From December until Spring, the high passes cradling Phoksumdo Lake are impenetrable, virtually cutting off the people remaining inside Dolpo from the rest of Nepal to the south.

On a world map, the kingdom of Nepal barely looks like a fold in the rising belly of southern Asia. Her total landmass is just over 56,000 square miles, only slightly larger than the state of Arkansas. Rising out of the plains of northeastern India, Nepal buttresses hillscapes that eventually surrender to the sacred mountains bordering Tibet, known to the people of Nepal as the "abode of the snows," the *Himalaya*.

The landscape is both the painter and the canvas of Nepali culture. Just as the mountains rise in stark contrast to the flatlands of the south, the lives of Nepal's people are diverse and entangled in paradox. Nepalis speak over thirty-five different languages stemming from

22

The land of Dolpo yields only fifty percent of the year's supply of grain, forcing locals to travel between the Hindu-speaking regions to the south and their native Tibetan-speaking regions further north.

the ancient cultures of Buddhist and pre-Buddhist Tibet, Aryan Hindu tribes of northern India, and the many indigenous settlements of the ancient *Gopal* and *Kirat* peoples.

It is only recently, since the national borders were officially opened in the 1950s, that Nepal has exposed itself to the outside world. The world

Traditionally traveling south in the winter and north into Tibet each summer, yak caravans carry supplies, salt and grain for trade.

was both shocked and awed by this rich weave of distinctive Asian cultures woven craftily into the land. The people's lives appeared both glorified and impoverished by an uncompromising reverence to the gods who rule an isolated and hidden land.

Spread across three main geographical regions of Nepal are variations on the

24

A Hindu home set among the flatlands of Lumbini, the birthplace of Lord Buddha. Athough Nepal's Terai *region marks the birthplace of the Buddhist faith, southern Nepal is inhabited primarily by Hindus and Muslims.*

Hindu and Buddhist faiths. Many Nepalis, although they claim to be a part of the 90% "Hindu" majority, nonetheless practice ancient forms of animistic worship, in which both spirits and many different mountain- and forest-dwelling deities are honored. In addition to Hindus and Buddhists, there are small Muslim communities throughout south and central

Nepal, as well as followers of Christian faiths, growing in number since Christian missionaries entered the country in the 1950s. Most of Tibetan Buddhist culture dwells in the *Himalaya*, following closely the traditions of neighboring Tibet, whereas Hindu populations reside primarily in Nepal's central hills and *Terai* plains, areas historically influenced by

An aging widow works in the rice fields of the Terai *region, just two miles from the border of eastern India. Although the region encompasses only 20% of Nepal's total landmass, the fertile soil and proximity to one of India's poorest states has made this southern strip the most populated region of the country, currently supporting over 50% of the population.*

Indians migrating from the south. Not surprisingly, between the mountains and the plains among the undulating hills of central Nepal are many syncretic ethnic groups whose faiths annex, or in some cases predate, the many varying beliefs of Buddhism and Hinduism.

For all of their differences, Nepali people share a profound sense of *dharma*. *Dharma* is a Sanskrit word translated most often as simply "religion." However, this definition falls short of all that *dharma* resonates in Nepali culture and what it impresses upon her people and their belief systems. *Dharma* embraces much. It is the imperative of moral responsibility, divine rule, religious merit, and pious actions. It has driven much of Nepali history, including the very

Nepal's middle hill communities sit between 2 and 12,000 feet in the outer Himalayan range. As altitudes change, so do ethnic and religious practices. The middle hills are home to many hybrid faiths, integrating Hinduism from the south, Buddhism from the north, and ancient animistic practices.

unification of what is now Nepal by King Prithvi Narayan Shah, who, in the eighteenth century, conquered and united the many tiny kingdoms of this ethnically scattered landscape in a divine quest to establish Hindu rule. The templescape of Nepal's cities and the thousands of ornately hand-carved wood- and mud-formed rest stops, *pipal* trees, and towering Buddhist *chortens* and mani walls on the rural and mountain trails are all monuments to deities and testament of the people's *dharma*. It is this drive for merit, to please and appease the varying Hindu, Buddhist, and animist deities, that bonds the collective conscience of the Nepali people. No matter which religious tradition one investigates, such con-

A deaf mountain girl carries yak dung in a bamboo doko basket strapped across her head.

science is not separated from the routine of daily life. Work is ritual worship. Survival is celebration.

It is the lay of the land more than ideology that divides and isolates the populations of Nepal. In fact, the country is home to one of the most prolific environments in the world. Twenty percent of Nepal's landmass lies in the Gangetic plains near India; its villages often sit in depressions just two hundred feet above sea level. Before the 1960s the *Terai* was virtually deserted by humans, its jungles infested with malaria and inhabited by an ethnic group known as the *Tharu* people who were remarkably resistant to the disease. With the near eradication of malaria, the *Terai* soon

28 *At 14,000 feet, a line of young women return to their high-altitude village. In the inner Himalaya, retrieving water may demand a two-hour walk; collecting purchased goods at a bazaar may be several days away.*

became a migration ground for hill and mountain people, as well as many impoverished farmers and tradesmen from neighboring India seeking opportunity in unsettled land. Today, the *Terai* holds over fifty percent of the Nepali population and, due to an open-border policy with India, its hybrid population continues to grow.

A nomadic yak herder returning home to inner Dolpo carries his granddaughter and food supplies inside his basket.

Overpopulation and a cycle of poverty now threatens the environment of these tropical jungle plains.

The *Terai* is predominantly inhabited by Hindus and Muslims who harvest mustard, rice, wheat, corn, herbs and fruit from what is Nepal's most fertile farm land.

30 *Children, along with weaving looms and daily wares, are carried along the arduous routes that many mountain families must travel. It is along the long trails south that many Tibetan-speaking mountain children hear their first words of the Nepali language. In order to facilitate trade and their potential to be educated, many mountain-dwelling children are now encouraged to learn Nepali.*

The middle hills of Nepal stretch the breadth of the country between the Indian states of Sikkim and Himalchal Pradesh. Also in the hills are tucked away rural valleys stretching up to nine and ten thousand feet. Here the predominant Gurung, Tamang, Rai and Limbu ethnic groups live atop terraced steppes in the rolling earth. Here is found Kathmandu,

In Kathmandu, a cow, considered sacred by Hindus, eats grain spread across the terrace of the city's ancient Durbar Square.

the capital city with a population of a million people, artisans as well as growing migrant and expatriate communities. The hill people are mainly farmers, extracting food from irrigated and terraced fields that are often only two or three rows wide, depending on the slope of the hillsides. Labor is intensive and survival is never certain for these people. As is also

true for their northern neighbors in the outer and inner *Himalaya*, water may be over a two-hour walk away. Carrying water becomes a routine job, usually reserved for women and children.

As one moves north towards Tibet, the land erupts into the *Himalaya*, the range of the tallest peaks in the world, including the tallest, Mt. Everest, at 29,028 feet. Lush

alpine valleys give way to forbidding and sacred peaks that unfold into plateau regions that are geographically associated with the expanse of Tibet. It is in these mountains that Nepal's ethnic groups gradually become more culturally—and in many cases economically—tied to the traditions of ancient Tibet and to the practices of Mahayana Buddhism. This inner

Moss and mustard flowers, Lumbini.

Himalayan mountain culture of the Sherpa, Manangi, Loba, Dolpo-pa, and Humli peoples is a world away from the dominant Hindu traditions, class-system and day-to-day life of those who live in Kathmandu, the middle hills, or the *Terai*. The mountain people have facial features that are more Mongolian, varying greatly from the Indo-Aryan features of the southern ethnic groups. Their languages, if not straight Tibetan, are of Tibeto-Burmese descent with writing that follows the Tibetan script. Many are semi-nomadic people, leaving their high-altitude settlements (often above 14,000 feet) after a once-yearly summer harvest of barley and pota-toe, to travel south with their herds of yak, sheep and trading goods to live and

A yak grazes in the valley of Langtang-Ri, 14,000 feet .

trade among the *Rong-Pa*, as the people of the south are known to the Tibetan-speaking. From November until March, elders, monastic communities, and those who otherwise choose not to make the migration south are locked beyond winter mountains of impenetrable ice.

It is this varying landscape that has given birth to and sustained Nepal's culture. Despite their diverse loyalties, the Nepali people seem linked by a strong and dependent relationship to their land and to the pan-cultural demands of survival. A World Bank study in 1990 estimated that of Nepal's nineteen million people, up to eight million live in "absolute poverty," their incomes below the level required to sustain the minimum calories needed for health. Geopolitics and geographical isolation, as well as a feudalistic class system that has flourished for centuries, have much to do with this economic poverty.

It is within this weave of Nepal's history, geography, ethnicity, and standard of survival that our story of deaf people begins.

*A child peers out the only window of
her home in Dolpo. Most high mountain
houses have no windows at all, to protect
against the winds and bitter cold.*

The Buddhas' Cave

The first major study on deafness in Nepal was undertaken by a group of medical doctors from Britain in 1990. From a sample population over the age of five, they found that 16.6% (2.71 million) of Nepali people are, to some degree, "deaf." Those who are "profoundly deaf," they said, compose a much lower 1.7%, although a report written by Deaf people of the Kathmandu Association of the Deaf in 1990 said that number was estimated at a much higher 3%. This estimate would indicate that over five hundred thousand of Nepal's nineteen million people are deaf. Though this is no doubt a relatively high fraction of the population compared with other, especially more developed, countries, it comes as no surprise to the people of Nepal. Most Nepali people know a deaf person, at least in their extended family, village, or community.

What the people of Nepal find more difficult to accept than sheer numbers and statistics on deaf people is that deafness does not discriminate; in fact it affects all ethnic groups, all castes and classes of people of each religion in Nepal. This is hard for Nepalis to come to terms with because deafness is considered a curse, an aggression

of one's own *karma*, a telltale sign of negative spiritual worth. To be deaf then, in a culture with such high standards of *dharma*, is a shame to the individual as well as to his or her family. Deafness is well hidden and quick to be disdained.

This makes assessing the number and conditions of deaf people in Nepal all the more problematic. In most areas of the

country, there is no single word that everyone understands that names a person who cannot hear. Deafness cannot be generally defined because no one seems to agree on what it is. Is it the wrath of God? The loss of hearing? Inability to speak? A temporary curse? Is it a condition of the spiritual makeup, the genetic makeup, or is it simply, like

Kept warm by woollen hats and tibetan-style chubas, these nomads rest after a long day's walk.

Three Buddhist brothers,
Kruk, upper Gorkha district

the blue of the sky, one's "fate" and not to be questioned any further?

The one word that is most associated with deafness is the derogatory name of *latto/latta*. The etymology of *latto* is best understood in its cultural context as the English equivalent of "dumb." Both words imply mute speech coupled with inherent stupidity. They have been misnomers for deaf people all over the world. The label *latto* is often used in jest to mimic the actions or words of an idiot, or to compare him to a useless guard dog who cannot bark. Most often, Nepalis do not separate being deaf from being stupid. To be deaf is considered by many to be less than human, useless, a burden and a shame in Nepali society. For higher caste families, a disabled family member mocks their whole premise of intellectual and spiritual superiority; for lower caste families, the embarrassment of deafness simply reinforces their low status and esteem.

In my search for deaf people across the rural areas of Nepal, people usually looked at me blankly when I asked if there were any *bhahiro* (deaf) people in their village. To most rural people, this is a formal and modern Nepali word that is of a foreign language. It was not until I said *kaan na sunnu sakne manche* (people whose ears do not hear) or *kura bolnu na sakne manche* (people whose mouths cannot speak) that the local faces would lighten up and they would laugh, *Ay! Latte-lai khojdaicha* (Oh! She's looking for 'dumb' people).

Because most pre-lingual[2] deaf people in Nepal have no formal education or means of acquiring language, what the Nepali people primarily notice of deaf people is that they cannot speak, that they are *latto*. Although they can perform menial survival tasks, as they mature with no bridge to the spoken world around them, their mental and emotional acculturation often lacks what is socially acceptable and normal. A *latto* is often true to his name because his behavior may be deviant, his speech only grunts and muted smiles, and his eyes filled with blankness and an unsettling stare. Moreover, because deaf people very often receive sub-standard care within the family, their physical development can be stunted and peculiar, thus further estranging them on a very impressionable level. Only a small portion of Nepalis have met an educated deaf person, visited a deaf club, seen a structured sign language, or simply ever been able to communicate with a profoundly deaf person. For most, there is no bridge into the world of deaf people.

Doing field research in the region of Dolpa, I took a well-educated deaf friend along with me. The common response among villagers was pointed fingers coupled with, "He doesn't look like a *latto*... He seems so clever." This made me wonder exactly how to define all that encompasses the word "deaf" in Nepal. Who composes the 16.6% of Nepali people who are hearing impaired? What forces are at work in their lives? Defining deafness is a journey into the culture, beliefs and value systems of these people. To take this journey, we must greet the landscape of their ex-

istence, acknowledge their neighborhood gods and goddesses and listen to the stories of their families. In doing so, we attempt to feel the subtle interplay of the divine, of survival, of all that is life in Nepal.

In my journeying across cultures I have come to realize that the word "deaf" means different things to different people. To define deafness is to create a

viewpoint for understanding and perceiving deaf people wherever one finds them. Naturally, the way in which one interacts with deaf people within a given culture, whether in the family setting, doctor's office, workplace, or not at all, will contribute to those perceptions.

The most popular Western perception of deafness is that which is medically

Child of a flower merchant, Pashupatinath, Kathmandu.

*Deaf people are as diverse as Nepal
itself. They represent the three main
religions, Hinduism, Buddhism and Islam
and each of the country's thirty-six
ethnic minority cultures.*

definable. It is the lack of hearing; the absence of one of the five senses granted by nature. A doctor, for example, is trained to see the deaf "patient" as a person in need, to detect what is "broken" and fix it. Backed by medical tradition and the forward march of science and technology, the doctor's aim is to alleviate "pain and suffering" by "curing" deafness.

But not all people, especially deaf people, would agree with this perspective. To many, deafness is not so much what it isn't, but what it *is*. In more developed countries, with the reaffirmation and formalization of sign language since the 1960s[3], deafness has undergone a transformation. Once a debilitating and institutionalizing disease, it has now become a distinguishing trait of humanity, to some, even an ethnicity.

For many deaf people, especially those in the relatively affluent West, being deaf means belonging to a namable culture, Deaf Culture. Deaf Culture has its own language, schools, arts, and way of looking at and synthesizing a relationship with the surrounding world. The fulcrum of this cultural view is anchored in the experiences of deaf people and their signed languages. Deaf Culture is currently being strengthened by recent laws that provide support services, educational alternatives, and equal rights for deaf people. For many deaf people, and those living and working closely with the deaf community in the United States, these days reflect a golden age of the Deaf experience. Just like the African-American or Native-American ethnic identity of today, many Deaf-Americans want their name in the pot, and in capitals, too.

These two views of deafness—the medical and the cultural—are, effectively, opposite. Using the ability to hear as a standard, the medically based perspective understands deafness as a pathology; it is the inability to hear, to know sound, and to speak natively as the primary means of communication. In this view, deafness is an enemy to be fought, a bacteria to outwit, helixes of DNA to be decoded. It is an antagonistic condition of the human body.

The Deaf Culture perspective sees deafness from a sociological and cultural perspective. To Culturalists, being deaf is not some mysterious phenomenon to be figured out and overcome. Rather, it is an identity to embrace, one based upon a visually expressed language complete with idiomatic expressions and a vocabulary based upon the experiences of deaf people. Now, due to generations of all-deaf families and a growing network among deaf people, Deafness is less considered a sickness. Finding a home in Deaf Culture, fewer Deaf people are choosing to conform their lives to a hearing world.

Such First World perspectives emphasize black and white. They polarize Deaf people from hearing people, and even Deaf people from other Deaf people. I have not found such polarities existing in Nepal. At least not yet. Nepali beliefs exist in the gray areas, within a montage of colorful myths and religious practices that provide the foundation

for the ways of the world. If all of Deaf world culture could be bound into a testament, Nepal's definition of the deaf experience could be Genesis. Theirs is the deafness men have known since before doctors or organized communities defined it; it is deafness decreed by the spirit world and its faithful disciples. Deafness in the Nepali version:

an aggression of the gods, a curse of the spirits, an evil spell, an unforeseen decree of supernatural wisdom.

Nepal is a land surviving upon the wealth of its myth, superstitions and folklore. It is the playground of thousands of Hindu and Buddhist deities and the one magnificent God of Islam, battling and frolicking amongst themselves as they

carry out their folly and spin the wheel of humankind. It is a land where science and technology have not yet found an explanation, an answer, or a challenge for every aspect of life; where people are defined according to their humanity and not their role as consumers; where the never-ending "whys" of children are not squelched with the black-and-white answers found in science textbooks and written constitutions, but instead are taken as invitations for folklore and story-telling, further embellished by personal experience. It is a land where mystery continues to unfold, and the human spirit still runs unabashedly after it.

With this sense of wonder the people of Nepal have come to define and under-stand deaf people. Knowing deafness means first going back to its source, which in Nepal usually has no understood con-nection with bacteria or disease, but with the whim of the gods and the justice they grant. In the same way that the modern religion of science battles and inexhaustibly strives to decode nature, the religious cul-ture of Nepal is constantly seeking deeper and deeper meanings of truth and causali-ty in the ever-turning cyclic wheel that is

their world. Deafness comes and goes in accordance with man's relationship to the spiritual world, not the biological and physical world. Divine interplay weighs more than scientific causality to the Nepali people; deafness is not some-thing they see in a microscope or as a factor of the genetic equation. Instead, they look to the moon and the stars or retreat into mountain caves to listen. The flow of the streams and the thick of the forests have much to tell, so the Nepalis refer to their environment as well as to the ancient texts of learned masters for clues of this world and how they might better understand their place within it.

Deafness has a place within this mystery. According to Nepali beliefs deaf-ness can come from many sources. Foremost is the belief in *karma* that could invite evil spirits to take away one's hear-ing. In the succession of lives through which both Buddhists and Hindus believe they will live and die, a deaf child is a living manifestation of low moral worth. From this perspective, deafness is most often understood as punishment, although teachers of *dharma* say it is more aptly

the "karmic justice" of existence. To be deaf is not simply the karmic aftermath of negative deeds from previous lives; it is divinely-inspired discipline, a lesson from supernatural forces designed to harness your wandering soul. Perhaps in your past life you gossiped too much and now the gods are dancing around your tongue withholding it from your use. Maybe you were a liar, you took what you heard and twisted it to your benefit. You could have previously been an animal and this is just one step forward in the ripening of your existence. *Karma* is more than "you get what you deserve"; to the Nepalis, *karma* is just, it is righteous, and it is for the ulti-mate benefit of all living beings and the betterment of the world.

To be deaf is not the only manifesta-tion of bad *karma*. Other disabilities, being born into a low caste, or what may appear as bad luck may be a further pub-lic testimony to the history and merit of one's soul. As a result, many Nepali people make no distinction among deafness, blindness, mental retardation, or other forms of disability or mental illness, as all are considered to arise from the same source, *karma*. Even better educated

people can wear holy blinders and associ-
ate deafness with being bad;
it is a way of separating oneself from
the other because, as one Nepali once
told me, "everyone needs someone
they can feel better than."

Even where such psychological
and religious rivets do not run so deep,
mythology and superstition still prevail.
In the Mustang district at a wintertime
festival of the Thakali people, I talked
to a man who had returned to his village
from the city for the once-in-every-
twelve-year festival.

*"Everyone knows 'latto' people don't
have tongues, that's why they can't talk,"*
he assured me while pointing to the six-
teen-year-old deaf mountain boy staring
blankly back at him. To this man there
was a simple, practical reason, free of
any ideological or moral judgment.

"But sir," I tried to sound as polite as
I could, *"I've known many deaf people in
my life, and they all had tongues in fact."*

*"They must have been foreigners. Here
in Nepal providence is different. These
lattos, their ears are fine. But they don't
have a tongue so, you see, they
have no capacity to communicate."*

I tried to explain, becoming more
adamant, but also thinking, "This man is
half right. At least he doesn't think that
deafness is just broken ears. At least he
can recognize the barriers." The deaf boy,
now looking completely aware of our
conversation, stood at our side evidently
amused as he watched our flailing
hands and heated debate.

The man spoke with such gentle,
pragmatic sincerity that my frustration
seemed inappropriate. Once I was sure
my words had failed to convince,
I hesitantly motioned to the deaf boy
to show us if his tongue was indeed there.
He opened his mouth and there it was,
red, just as everyday looking as everything
else on his invisibly deaf body. The man

*Mountain Buddhist
Tseten Dolma Lama eating*
dal-bhaat, *traditional
Nepali rice and lentils.*

Limbu children in a doorway, Taplejung

just looked in disbelief, thirty-five years of his own village wisdom denied.

I have been given many other explanations for deafness as well. Aside from the fundamental belief that deaf ears are simply part of one's karmic make-up, there are supposed special factors in creating deafness. Evil spirits present at conception or birth, inter-caste marriage, the wrath of a *bon-jhankri* (forest spirit), or other inexplicable interplays of supernatural forces can all take part in the creation of a deaf child. The piercing of the ears on newborn boys and girls across most of Nepal verifies the faith in the old wives' tale that deafness can strike if you fail to do so. It is also said that if an expecting mother has too much sex during pregnancy, her child will be unhealthy and, very possibly, deaf. I once read the biography of an elder Nepali woman from the hills who spoke of the people who have become deaf from *"having the net that is inside their ear broken by the sound of lightning."*[4]

From the holistic tradition of Eastern medicine comes the explanation that deafness is essentially due to ancestral or genetic chi (lifeblood and energies). Ayurvedic medicine further warns that mixing pork, beef, mutton or fish with honey, molasses, sesame, milk, black lentil or radish will also lead to deafness over time.[5]

Because of the spiritual associations with the causes of deafness, Nepalis look to similar sources of wisdom for actions to prevent such a condition. Most common among many ethnic groups across Nepal is the wearing of charms (written prayers, conch shells, and auspicious stones) around the neck to ensure good health by warding off evil spirits. Nepalis on the whole also pay much respect to their local healers, *dhamis, jhankris* and *bijuwas*, who, via their learned connections with the supernatural, can sustain favor with the gods and thus protect families and individuals from deafness.

A Gurung Hindu porter and a traveling Buddhist pilgrim meet on a high mountain trail, in a relaxed exchange of affection.

Until perhaps twenty-five years ago, every household of the Limbu tribe in the eastern hills of Nepal had a shrine to the folk god *Bhimsen Devta,* who was believed to protect families from deafness. As with all Eastern healing methods once inseparably woven into the local religious culture, such worship and appeasement of deities is now being marginalized by the influx of Western-trained Nepali doctors and their allopathic medicine.

Yet long before Western allopathic medicine and its technologies arrived in Nepal, the indigenous people had their own medicinal materials for treating deafness. The *Gharuva* healers of the Tharu tribe in the lower breadth of Nepal use the commonly found jungle plant *chlorodendium biscosum* for curing deafness and complications of the ear. The ancient medicine man Charak, who wrote the famous ayurvedic text *Charak Samhita* over 2,000 years ago, believed that the juice of this commonly found plant from the forests of the *Terai* was an effective herbal remedy for deaf people. The urine of the one-horned rhinoceros, although very expensive, is also believed to be a sure remedy for hearing complications. In hopes of stumbling across a fortune, locals routinely carry plastic bags with them while traveling through the jungle in the event they should find a urinating rhino.

44

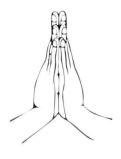

Three Buddhist Ngakpa lay monks of Tibetan Buddhism's oldest sect temporarily erect their tent in the forests of a "Hidden Valley" in Nepal's northern Himalayan region. Trusted as teachers and learned scholars, this father and his two sons are often called upon to share their knowledge of spiritual healing methods.

Healers of the Spirit

Three deaf men come seeking a "cure" at a mountain-relief medical camp. The two older men have been deafened late in life and both happen to be ethnic Limbu Dhamis, spiritual healers. After their own self-healing methods failed, they are willing to attempt allopathic Western medicines.

Perhaps a more popular treatment than anything taken internally is the spiritual medicine that Nepalis believe only the gods can give. The moment a child is suspected of being deaf, he or she is taken to the local *jhankri* (healer and priest), who will conduct a series of rituals to cast out evil spirits believed to be inhabiting the body. Although such rituals are focused around the time deafness is first discovered, efforts to cast out deafness are often continued throughout a person's life.

Others in the Kathmandu Valley only treat deafness until the age of five. Many Hindu parents take their deaf son or daughter on ritual visits to the *Surya Binayak* temple above the ancient city of Bhaktapur. Belief has it that the child's irrevocable fate will manifest itself within five years. If the gods do not withdraw their curse within that time, then deafness is presumed to be for life.

Varying attempts to heal demonstrate the intercultural dynamic and syncretic traditions of Nepal's many ethnic tribes and religious cultures. Although local

46 *Wrapped in his traditional white cloth, Baba Devi Prasad Paudel, a Hindu Brahmin Priest from the southern Terai region, travels for his first time into the Buddhist mountain communities of Dolpo, in search of deaf people. Away from the predominant Hindu social orthodoxy of the south that deems Buddhist people "unclean," he accepts a hand extended by a new Buddhist friend from Dolpo.*

healers may have different methods, all spritual efforts ultimately must face the divine, seeking to appease and exorcise spirits. I have met Hindus who, after "trying everything" for their deaf child, faithfully go to the Tibetan Buddhist *amche* (doctor) in a neighboring village higher in the *Himalaya*. Nomadic Buddhists will stop and see the *Bon* (pre-Buddhist, animist) shaman on their biannual descent into the lower lands to see if he can affect their fate.

More recently, traditional rural people have begun to wander into Kathmandu clad in leopard-lined *chubas*, or with bangles from their knees to their ankles, in bare feet adorned with checkerboard tattoos. They carry their babies tied in a knotted blanket on their back, ready to try the allopathic remedies of a European science they have yet to understand. Yet I have talked to middle- and upper-class urban elites who admit that they returned to the rural village of their grandfathers in search of a healer who might do what no M.D. in Kathmandu could.

A Buddhist Lama stands outside his one-room temple in a Dolpo village. Also trained as an amche, a traditional Tibetan doctor, dried medicinal herbs in animal skin bags hang from his door.

There is a sense of ritual comforting that only traditional doctors can give to Nepalis. A well-educated Nepali filmmaker who has made many documentaries on aspects of culture and survival in the Himalaya once told me that local healers, shamans, *jhankris*, *lamas*, and priests are the strongest source of emotional support for village culture. Even if families do seek Western medicine in their attempt to cure deafness, they often fall back on the invested powers of the local healer as well. The ritual aspect of healing is such that it can be a form of worship for many Nepalis. A *jhankri* from eastern Nepal has told me the same. Even when he knows he can do nothing for a deaf child, he still welcomes the family, performs *puja*, and invokes certain spirits. "After all," he said, " it is their way of life as well as my livelihood."

In rural Nepal, these healers are trusted and respected wise men. Both Buddhists and Hindus visit these men, who conduct various rituals and exorcisms, usually to reverse bad fortune or heal illness. I recognize these men as

Dr. Yanta Mani Pradhan travels by Twin-Otter plane, four-wheel drive, horseback, and on foot with his medical teams into some of Nepal's harshest and most remote regions. Although many patients flock to his camps with ear and respiratory infections, these are the most difficult to treat.

true experts on the hearts and minds of Nepali people. They are confided in and see close up their people's fears of the unknown.

Although it is the family that most often suspects a person's hearing or speech difficulties, it is the *jhankri* who confirms deafness and makes it real to them. Thanks to some growing awareness of deaf education, *jhankris* are more often taking an active social role in the aftermath of detection. In eastern Nepal, I spoke with two *jhankris*, one of whom was nearing profound deafness in his old age. These local healers live in a very difficult time; through our conversation, I could see that they must now try to balance the old ways with the new if they

are to keep their profession and tradition alive. Nepal is changing very fast. People's beliefs and support systems are being tested by exposure to the outside world, and traditions are rapidly undergoing an inevitable and awkward transformation. Local healers and shamans are absorbing these changes. Although they are still more trusted in the villages than allopathic medical doctors, they know their time is fading. When their own methods and charms fail, they often send people off to the cities in search of the rich man's medicine.

I interviewed several *jhankris* who had come seeking assistance at a medical camp set up in the hill station of Taplejung near the border of Sikkim. One explained to me:

A local Hindu jhankri, in the mountains of eastern Nepal conducts an exorcism. Using red and white flowers as an offering, the shaman calls upon the spirit of a deaf person and takes it into his own body. The ritual is a way, he says, "to bring back honor to a person who has been disgraced."

I walk with all the worries of humans. Deaf people come to us. . . we chant to the gods, feed them and put different herbs and plants around them. If this doesn't cure them then we send them immediately to the health post.

There are a lot of ears that don't hear and blindness from village to village. For this treatment we do as much as we know, calling to gods and goddesses, making water medicines. This is how we keep trying and trying. . . to be "latto," without arms or legs, this [the disabled people] have brought from birth. When we can do nothing to make the lattos' ears to hear, and they come back from the health posts and doctors' offices [in the local cities] and Kathmandu and still cannot use their voice, then we know that they were meant to be like this.

Next to him sat another local *jhankri,* who is becoming deaf himself, who spoke of his own experience with deafness, the limitations of his own methods, and his willingness to accept alternatives in a changing world.

Thirty years ago I began doing jhankri work, and for twelve years my ears have been closed. After my ears closed, I treated myself differently. I requested to all the gods and goddesses to whom I respect, but this has not had any effect on me. I even let other witch doctors and shamans do things for me, but nothing was found and no meaning has come of all this.

Since then, I have thought, "this is not punishment from the deities." So I have

50 *A Hindu ethnic Brahmin brings his eleven-year-old deaf son to a remote mountain medical camp in hopes of "curing" him.*

come now to be examined by a big officer doctor. Either my eardrum is broken or there is dust sitting in my ear. . . for whatever they have to clean, for whatever they have to do, I have come to be examined.

Deafness perplexes both local healers and outside doctors. The medical profession in Nepal can neither sufficiently tackle the complications of deafness nor provide explanations for its prevalence better than traditional wisdom and healers. Although a 1990 medical survey shows that nearly seventeen percent of the Nepali population is "hearing impaired," it is not understood why or how they are deaf, where these people live, or further, how to reach them. Just as people dying from "natural" causes in the *Himalaya* could actually be suffering from undiagnosed cancer or high blood pressure, so children are developing a variety of unnamed illnesses that could be causing hearing trauma.

The medical professionals can say that twenty-one percent of hearing impairment is caused by the bacterial infection *otitus media*. Studies have shown that this infection affects fifty-six percent of

Nepali school children. Commonly known as "glue ear," *otitus media* infects the middle ear by way of dirty water, and lack of sanitary conditions and bathing, and is clearly detectable by the constant presence of a white, glue-like pus sitting in the outer ear cavity. It is very often found coupled with the chronic runny noses so typical of children living in high-altitude mountain areas, but is by no means exclusive to the mountain people.

Trekking in a low-elevation hill area at 9,000 feet, I came across a woman holding a young girl's head in her lap. With a small stick the size of a ballpoint pen, she was probing one inch inside of the child's ear. When I asked her what she was doing, she said she was cleaning out the foul-smelling *peep* (pus) that drips out of her daughter's ear and onto her clothes every day. Although she was obviously trying to remedy the situation, it is this common practice of putting foreign objects inside the ear that causes such infections in the first place. Such ignorance and deplorable health standards are commonplace. The medical field laments the fact that sixty-one percent of Nepalis do not (or cannot) go to a health post for treatment of

51

"Most people think deafness is a result of their bad karma," explains Nepali doctor Yanta Mani Pradhan. *"In fact, the deafness here mostly comes from infection, typhoid fever, meningitis, tuberculosis injections, and overdoses of malaria medicine."* This hard-of-hearing school child suffering from a painful "glue ear" infection sits in a Kathmandu valley school house awaiting a prescription by Dr. Pradhan. He wears an amulet around his neck to protect him from the evil spirits that may worsen his sickness.

"Deafness is not only a medical treatment problem, it is a social challenge as well in our society," *says Dr. Pradhan. School boys await eye and ear checkups by the doctor.*

infection and disease, making the challenge of their jobs even more overwhelming. Over one-third of all the deafness in Nepal, they say, is preventable.

Perhaps more telling is a 1981 UNICEF study that found a correlation between disabilities and poverty. It is most often the poorer rural populations across the country who have the least access to medical attention and education. Language differences also complicate this situation. Because few of those in the ethnic minority can read or write, and some have no common language with other Nepalis, they are cut off not only from their government, but also from each other.

In cases of gradual hearing loss over time due to infection and disease, it is the more remote or impoverished people who can least afford the time and money necessary to arrest their condition. Vaccinations, what few are available, seldom reach these communities. Typhoid and meningitis, both common preludes to acquired deafness, are still widespread. In the mountains especially, water can be a couple of hours away. In cities, water is likely to be infested with bacteria and

Many Nepalis liken a doctor trained in modern medicines to a God. Their prescribed pills and ointments often produce quick and drastic results, producing what seems nothing short of a "miracle" to the locals. In this case, Dr. T. B. Dahal can do nothing but provide this mountain boy with antibiotics and a pain reliever for the chronic ear infection that has already made him profoundly deaf.

many people cannot afford (or do not know) to filter and boil it before drinking. What hospitals do exist are overcrowded, and the government-funded free beds may have a waiting list of a couple of years—enough time for a simple ear infection to become permanent deafness. It is often the poorer and rural communities that suffer from iodine deficiency and cretinism, chronic bacterial infections such as glue ear, and the lack of medical services that could otherwise detect deafness in a person's crucial youngest years.

Although Nepal does have people who are born congenitally deaf, there appears to be a higher proportion of those deafened due to childhood disease and later medical complications. This makes deafness seem that much more a pathology, a "sickness," and a disabling condition for the people living with it within families and communities. These conditions fuel a complicated cycle for families with disability and explain why deafness is most often perceived as a tremendous burden in Nepali society.

54

Surgery in the mountains requires a monumental effort. To reach the neediest communities, Dr. Yanta Mani Pradhan and his team often walk days carrying diesel generators, fuel, sterilization equipment, fragile surgical instruments and infection-fighting medicines into remote mountain villages. Seldom do they find the resources of a district hospital; operation rooms are most often set up in temples, school rooms, and homes.

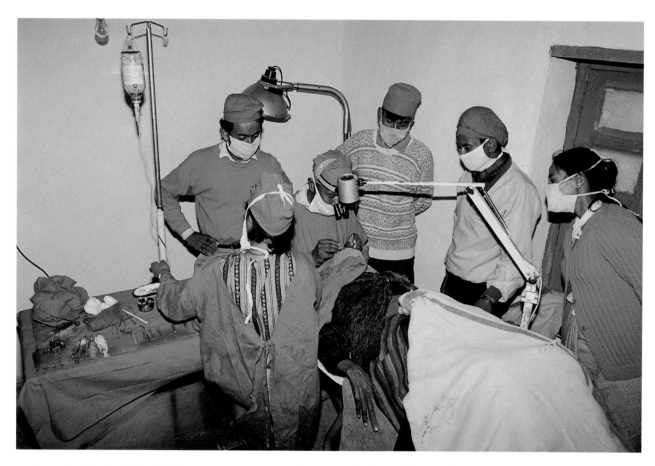

By contrast, in the United States today, a higher percentage of the deaf population is born deaf. Individuals suffer fewer complications coupled with, or leading to, their hearing loss. In the United States there is greater opportunity to look beyond simply the "broken" aspect of deaf people's lives. Affluence, basic health care, and educa-

tion are so much more easily obtainable by deaf people in the West, allowing them self-reliance, as well as the time and leisure to innovate new ways to shape public perception of who they are. Today, some members of the American Deaf Community are insulted at medical efforts to "prevent" deafness. I often wonder how their reactions might change

if they could understand the lives of their deaf peers in the Third World.

In Nepal, being deaf is more than just a game of genetic roulette. It can be the aftermath of a long and painful disease; it can come after just one night of a mysterious, frightening, hallucinating fever; or it can be a gradually worsening condition that makes deaf children the brunt

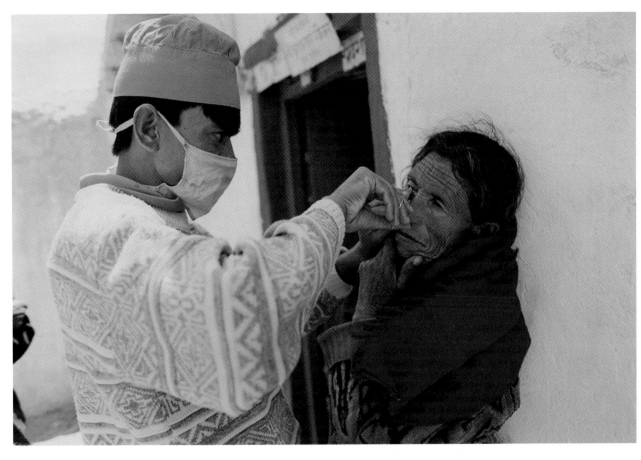

In preparation for cataract surgery, volunteer medical technician Ram Bahadur Kumar removes a blind woman's eyelashes.

of ridicule and hardship throughout their development. Such possibilities, along with the sure stigma cast upon deaf people, make Nepalis fear deafness. It is a looming nightmare for parents, a potential embarrassment for a family, and a real threat to the many children all across the country that are suffering from disease .

Regardless of how one defines what deafness is, the fact remains that some Nepali deaf children are dying from complications related to their deafness. Too many families, especially in rural and isolated areas, cannot afford allopathic medical treatment. The result is that sinus and ear infections not only deafen Nepalis over time, but may kill them.

The medical field is clearly frustrated by the enormity of their challenge.

Dr. Yanta Mani Pradhan, a Nepali eye, ear, nose and throat surgeon who leads medical teams in remote medical camps, once told me, *"Even my deaf patients I treat differently from the others. It's so easy to communicate with my eye patients, but the deaf person can't tell me what the problem is nor understand what I am trying to say."* I have walked days with

him, his crews and his equipment, to meet both deaf and blind people in high-elevation settlements at hill-station health posts, and I discern his sincerity. Without a formal means to communicate with deaf people and the proper equipment, Dr. Pradhan can usually do little for those who have walked for days seeking a cure for their ears.

Traveling from his village to a medical camp a days' walk away, an aging blind man is carried by a local porter in a makeshift doko basket.

From a Nepali medical standpoint, working with deaf patients is relatively time-consuming and does not yield much result or cure. Ear surgery tools and microscopes are extremely expensive, as well as delicate, and too easily break when transported into remote areas. Doctors are already overburdened in the cities and most feel they can not take the time to volunteer their services at medical camps. Further, with the harsh relative perspective that so many critical-care doctors must have in their work, many deaf people are doing better than most other "sick" Nepalis. With the exception of those who have serious health problems related to their hearing loss, deaf Nepalis are relatively able-bodied and, even if suffering from a painful ear infection, can still work along with everyone else. A doctor must prioritize and balance efforts. Despite Dr. Pradhan's dedication to deaf people and their need to be educated, his hands ultimately heal more immediately curable ills.

Dr. Pradhan and others must consider many factors when deciding who they can treat on their tight schedules. In the life-and-death situations found at medical

camps, a deaf child can wait at the end of the line; the child dying from diarrhea or typhoid cannot (and yet, fatally, often does). I have heard an exasperated, *"We can hardly accommodate the "normal" children, how can you expect us to reach all the deaf as well?"* That feeling is not just from medical workers, but from educators, religious leaders, and foreign aid workers as well.

Although such sentiments stigmatize deaf people as being "abnormal" and at the end of the nation's developmental priority list, arguing such points treads on sensitive ground. Statistics of poverty and disability along with the logistical difficulties of reaching most of the Nepali people are very real. Many efforts to help deaf citizens are still being jump-started, and many are being made for the first time. There are bound to be mistakes, including the temptation to fall back on old ways, which often seem safer and more secure than the new. It is hard to see the direction this development will take. However, to know where the Nepali people are going, it is essential to understand first where they have been.

A Sherpa widow at her home in Helambu.

Caught in the Wheel

Buddhists from a high-altitude village greet an oncoming Buddhist priest with traditional reverence.

In Nepal's isolated ethnic communities, attitudes and social norms have developed and anchored themselves in ways of life that sustain the community over many seasons. The people of Nepal are not quick to change their ways, as change is often a gamble with life while living on the frontier of survival. In many respects, the wealth of beliefs and tra-

ditional knowledge compose the social infrastructure; there is no advanced technology for material improvement, no bank loans or food reserves to fall back on in hard times. To maintain traditional ways is to maintain life.

Here, interdependency is the rule. Unlike the deaf communities of the West whose members can enjoy relative auton-

omy in both the cultural and the economic spheres, the lives of most Nepali deaf people cannot be separated from the country's hearing majority. Although there are three major religions, thousands of varying and competing gods and goddesses, and histories and cultural traditions unique to specific regions, within this diversity resonates a greater cultural

60

Dudrupchen Rinpoche, a venerable Buddhist teacher from Bhutan, is flown from Kathmandu to a mountain village by helicopter. In his honor, local men wait anxiously to carry him to a gompa high in the mountains where he will conduct a continuous month-long puja ritual for the well-being of the Buddhist community.

rhythm: survival. It binds the mountains to the plains and, oftentimes, the castes and classes of the Nepali people to one another. Survival has defined the perimeters of mystery and belief, of being Nepali. Within these boundaries lies a common understanding of deaf people.

There is one fundamental belief that the people of Nepal share concerning their existence, their life and death; it is the distinguishing factor that many Westerners label as "Eastern." It is the concept of rebirth and the law of *karma* that reside within both Hinduism and Buddhism. In the walk of this life, and of the many lives Hindus and Buddhists believe they will journey through, *karma* can be thought of as the only luggage one will ever take. Only *karma* transcends death and carries onwards after rebirth; it can never disappear, only ripen, as our souls harvest life after life. All else—material objects, friends, one's environment, the physical form, be it human or otherwise—is impermanent and will change face, manifesting anew with each successive life.

Karma literally means "action," but it has come to imply much more in the way it is interpreted, both in the East and in

the West. *Karma* is not just action, but the power latent within our actions. It is also the end result our actions may bring. For most people of Nepal, it is essentially the law of cause and effect that governs their universe; it is a simple, yet ultimate, justice. The Nepali's faith in *karma* is similar to the endowment of trust many Westerners place in the biblical verse "As you sow, so shall ye reap." This what-goes-around-comes-around belief rewards virtuous acts with merit and moral integrity, and harmful or selfish acts with demerit and punishment. Sogyal Rinpoche, a teacher of the Tibetan Buddhist tradition, describes it:

In simple terms, what does karma *mean? It means that whatever we do, with our body, speech, or mind, will have a corresponding result. Each action, even the smallest, is pregnant with its consequences. It is said by the masters that a little poison can cause death, and even a tiny seed can become a huge tree.*[6]

Furthermore, *karma* can apply not just to individuals but to communities and geographical locations as well. It can be the sum of its many parts, applying to a whole nation and the combined *karma* of its people. It is possible then for a community to have "good *karma*"–a thriving economic base, good health, punctual rains, all set in a bountiful landscape; or "negative *karma*"–onslaught of disease, drought, crop failure, or a cluster of deafness for that matter.

Accordingly, if an individual person has negative *karma*, this would suggest that bad deeds have been done in the past, whether in a previous life or just yesterday. Every action has a reaction, and the human condition is often an indicator, a telltale sign of the virtue of previous lives. Sakyamuni Buddha, the founder of the Buddhist faith, said, *"What you are is what you have been, what you will be is what you do now."* With respect to the future, his great learned saint Padmasambhava adds, *"If you want to know your future life, look at your present actions."*[7] Deafness in karmic terms, then, is a manifestation of the evolution of the soul. To be deaf indicates both where one has been and where one is going.

61

In Nepali families, a disabled child can magnify the stresses that already exist in their day-to-day life. Out of Bhikan Musselman's eight children, four are deaf. "What can I do? What can I say? This is God's wish. This is God's happiness."

A young mother carries her sick infant in the Jumla district. Of those under five years in Jumla, 30% will die each year from diarrhea, pneumonia, measles, and other diseases.

Unfortunately, *karma* is easily misunderstood and misused in its definition. It is the self-serving misuses of karmic law, not the true justice that it intends to illuminate, that have been harmful to deaf people. In the West, people too easily understand *karma* as fate or predestination: "what will be, will be." Easterners can just as quickly alter understandings of karmic law for their own benefit. One's karmic fate is often used to legitimize inaction or wrongdoing, and most Nepali people hesitate to "interfere" with *karma*, as they claim this would be an arrogant breach of faith with the gods. People may therefore use another's *karma* as an excuse not to lend a helping hand, fatalistically saying that whatever others suffer, it is "their *karma*" to do so.[8] These manipulated interpretations of *karma* betray the integrity of deaf people and constrain their opportunities, not just in Nepal, but in other countries that also embrace such beliefs.

To a large extent the laws of *karma* have been institutionalized in Nepal through the caste system, the vertical social hierarchy legitimized by tenets of Hindu belief. Originally descending from the ancient laws of *Manu* compiled as divine revelation by *Brahmin* priests of India, the caste system was first installed in Nepal in the sixteenth century. Because one's family and caste dictate many Nepalis' line of work and place in the social ladder, daily life and routines of caste are considered a testament to karmic worth.

In the traditional model, the caste system is made up of four levels, each with an ideological equivalent to a portion of the human body. One's level pertains to the work expectations of that particular caste. In order, from highest to lowest in prestige, they rank: *Brahmin* (priest caste, related to the head), *Kshatriya* (warrior or administrator caste, related to the arms), *Vaisya* (merchant caste, related to the legs), and *Shudra* (labor caste, related to the feet). Finally, *Untouchables* are those who are not considered to be within the caste system and are, therefore, pariahs.

A society that places faith in such a divine decree of social organization believes that everything, and everyone, will fall into place according to the wisdom of the gods. The deities can see from the beginning of time into the infinite. Based upon this vision and wisdom, they can create the blueprint of lives that will enable the best functioning of society. To question such divine law is blasphemous, and, until Nepal created a democracy in 1990, it was illegal as well.

For Nepal, the caste system is effectively the laws of *karma* enforced and legitimized by the Hindu majority, tailored to sustain a workable society. For centuries, Nepali people lived under a series of "divine" autocrats, each successive national king considered to be a reincarnation of the mighty Hindu God Vishnu. With the exception of high-altitude Himalayan communities, political and social leaders were almost always of high-caste Hindu descent.

Across all of Nepal, there has long been a strong and symbolic tie between parent and child, this relationship outweighing the more popular Western notion of individualism, individual merit, and virtue. Even the Rana family, who ruled Nepal for over 100 years until 1950, did not officially recognize any personal talent, ability or academic achievement; only proper parentage could provide opportunity for social

Nepalis are bound together in their reverence towards both benevolent and wrathful deities. This Buddhist woman recites mantras (ritual chants) before undergoing surgery to protect her from harm.

advancement. This tie is also applicable in reverse. When parents give birth to an "imperfect" child, they feel a stigma and often will go to the extent of covering up the imperfection or disguising the relationship. Many deaf children are orphaned for this reason. If kept within the family, the child may be made to work as a servant to whom the family may claim no relation at all.

Ishwori is a seventeen-year-old deaf woman who was born into a high-caste family. She has lived her life in and out of foster homes and orphanages in Kathmandu. She told me her story:

I don't know my real family (caste) name. Why is that? A long time ago when I was a little girl, I didn't even

know what caste I was. Was I Newar? Brahmin? I didn't know. Now I have grown up and have since found out that I am Chettri.

I once asked the sister at the orphanage, "Where are my mother and father?" And she told me that when I was a baby they left me on the side of the road. I must have been an ugly little girl, or maybe my skin was too dark for their liking. Maybe it was because they knew I was deaf... That must be why they put me on the side of the road. What else can I say?

However objectionable it may be, on a pragmatic level the caste system has provided a basic foundation for Nepali society. Where there is no formal access to education, caste serves to pass down skills and training needed by society and as a means for individuals to make a living. Traditionally, a son will follow in his father's occupation and a daughter will marry into a caste close or equal to her family's in social privilege. Consistent with the bodily equivalents of their caste, the higher castes generally tend to perform work associated with the head and hands, whereas the lower castes perform more physical labor with their legs and feet. Society is stratified in such a way that one must engage in activities that are appropriate to one's caste. A *Brahmin* will not become a shoemaker (working with the feet and the leather of the sacred Hindu cow) just as a butcher's son

will not aspire to be a priest. From birth, children are conditioned by both their parents and the attitudes of the society around them to stay within the confines of their caste's prescribed role.

Deaf people, however, are usually considered low caste, regardless of their family name or background. Even those born to higher castes are relegated to low-caste status due to societal bias against their presumed *karma*. With lives complicated by communication barriers, deaf Nepalis are often delegated to the physical labor associated with the lower castes. Such work, many Nepalis believe, is necessary for the accumulation of merit in order to advance to a better social position in later lives. Deaf people, much like low-caste people, are

In the animistic Hindu region of Dolpa, this Maatwaali Chettri dresses in a woman's sari in a reverent festival dance.

An animistic deity carved from a sacred tree lies along a path in Dolpo.

supposedly in need of such merit-building responsibility. They are most often expected to spend their lives atoning for their souls.

These beliefs are not so strong everywhere in Nepal. Especially among the Buddhist communities and in more rural hill and mountain areas, survival demands a flexibility that loosens this caste structure and brings deaf people more closely into the circle of survival. Work becomes less of a status symbol or a religious role and more a vehicle for living. Cooperation and interdependency are necessary to get many villages through harsh winters or times of drought. At such times, the structures of caste are loosened in exchange for survival.

Because of the religious variation among the scattered Nepali population, as well as the autonomy of ethnic communities throughout Nepal's history, the traditional caste system is not as strong as it is in neighboring India. Especially in the context of an increasingly modern Nepal, there is a more secular interpretation of caste, one that has effectively become a class system with the politically or economically powerful on top

and the common poor and socially backward, usually rural and mountain peoples, at the bottom.

Ethnicity is the most distinguishing feature of Nepali people, and communities are labeled by their ethnic name, like *Newar* (originally of the Kathmandu Valley) or *Sherpa* ("people from the East [of Tibet]"), although these names are not formally of Hindu caste origin. Rural peoples, especially *Bhoteys*, as people of Tibetan descent are often called, are considered low class and low caste by the Hindu majority. Even though they sit at the bottom rung of the mainstream social ladder, these people observe their own class structure, not all too different from the whole notion of caste.

In the Tibetan communities of the *Himalaya*, although not formally following the Hindu-decreed divine origin of castes, there is very strong emphasis placed on family lineage, one that usually determines economic, marital, and monastic or educational opportunity. Areas like the high *Himalaya* are more closely linked with an autonomous Tibetan culture that enforces its own levels of social status and, interestingly, whose higher classes

A young water buffalo and goat lie beheaded in Kathmandu's main temple square. During the Dasain festival each autumn, Hindus attempt to appease the wrathful Goddess Durga by offering a blood sacrifice.

can be wealthier than even the highest caste families in nearby Hindu communities. To the high mountain dwellers, the Hindu caste division is merely a state-formulated structure that loses hold, and relevance, as it travels further and further into the remote mountain areas. It is only in the presence of other Hindus, or in the incidence of migration to the cities or lowland areas, that these Tibetans become perceived as low caste. In either case, whether one is Hindu or Buddhist, one's worth comes from the condition of one's birth. Across Nepal, the conclusion about a deaf person is that he or she is "meant to be that way." Such a brand does more than just strike against one's social status. It can be a strike against survival.

The importance that Nepalis place on one's birth and karmic destination has bred over centuries a deeply ingrained sense of fatalism. Fatalism implies that neither individuals nor communities of people have control over their circumstances. Everything is determined by supernatural and divine forces. This idea is supported by and executed through the caste and class systems of Nepal. Whether bestowing their gifts or their wrath, the gods decree the fate of the world. Their wisdom supersedes human limitations, so to question why things occur as they do, to demonstrate individualistic aspirations, or to provide humanitarian or altruistic assistance to the lower strata of society (aside from what is

religiously prescribed for the beggar caste) is to defy divinely inspired plans.

In their daily talk, Nepalis will often allude to myths illustrating such beliefs. For example, Brahmanistic Hindus anticipate that on the sixth night after a child's birth, *Bhavi*, the demi-god of providence, comes to write the fate of the newborn child on its forehead. *Bhavi's* writings reveal the pre-mapped *karma* of the child, and it is not possible to alter one's *bhagya* (fate) unless certain rituals are performed by *Brahmin* priests (for a fee). These rituals aim to redirect supernatural forces. In reference to this, many Nepalis will often slap their forehead with the back of their hand while saying "One cannot have what one sees, only what is written [on the forehead]."[9] Even non-

"We first knew she was deaf when we would call her name and she would not come to us," says a worried father of his five-year-old daughter. In their mountain village of Jhankot, an estimated 25% of the children are deaf.

Hindus often have sincere beliefs of karmic determination and will take their deaf child (or deafened adult) to a local priest, who will then make an effort to contact certain spirits in order to reverse whatever "curse" has befallen their family or to ask that they be pardoned from such karmic punishment. Such rituals, or *pujas*, may be carried on throughout the life of a deaf person in hopes of reversing this "curse."

The relationship between different communities and castes of the Nepali people is shaped by their fatalistic beliefs. Dor Bahadur Bista, a Nepali anthropologist and author, looks inside his own high-caste culture and says:

Charity is not valued under Hinduism— charity being strongly distinguished from giving alms to the holy. Altruism is suspect. Similarly one is never obliged to anyone for anything because everything occurs as it should. No sense of obligation is instilled. When a priest receives a gift, he never thanks the giver. It is the giver, the client, who should be thanking the priest for accepting it, for in accepting it the priest bestows spiritual merit on the giver. Though there are ways of expressing gratitude, "thank you" does not exist in the Nepali vocabulary and a new word, "dhanyabad," has been coined recently as the translation of the English "thanks."[10]

Because both Hindus and Buddhists believe that human life is ultimately painful illusion, it is common for Nepalis to focus their attention upon the afterlife and the ritualistic merits that can speed them along into a higher life form in later lives. When the underprivileged communities embrace such beliefs it does serve to distract them from their poor living conditions, but it can also stagnate their motivation for self-help. It is not unusual for *Brahmin* priests to tell poor, suffering, or disabled people who come to them that they are the "chosen ones" of God and that He wishes them to remain poor so that they can remain devoted to Him.[11] Although deaf people themselves do not necessarily follow such a sense of fatalistic discipline, their families often do, and as a result are confined within this mentality of dutiful and noble suffering.

This deaf girl was found in her village and brought to a deaf boarding school. Her case is rare; when rural families are given the opportunity to educate a child, it is least often a daughter, much less a deaf daughter.

70

Chejzum Motharra, a deaf Buddhist, sits outside a Bon (pre-Buddhist) temple in Dolpa. According to villagers, she knows no formal sign language and uses only crude hand gestures to communicate. She is married to a deaf man and they have four hearing children.

Although some Nepalis of today are struggling to live in exile from traditional religious life, the culture of fatalism still encompasses most of Nepal's communities. It is perhaps the women of Nepal who carry the weight of this ancient culture, especially in the mainstream Hindu communities where most women are traditionally bound to men in order to get along. Although the Hindu act of *suttee* (when women must lay down on the burning cremation pyre to die along with their husband) has been banished in both India and Nepal, in today's Nepal many higher caste women are still not allowed to walk outside alone without a family male escort. Some still ritually wash the feet of their husband each morning, and their tradition conditions them to worship their fathers, brothers, and, ultimately, their husbands. In the case of deaf women, their relationship with the society around them is even more dependent. They are caught in a downward spiral with no tools to free themselves. To endure the complications of a woman's life with little or no communication makes a Nepali deaf woman the epitome of the underprivileged.

Because it is considered a deaf person's fate to work hard, they are expected to do so without expectation of result or reward, except for survival. The Hindu caste principle states that actions and caste responsibilities must be done without desire; there is purpose to action, but it is a purpose known exclusively by the gods or supernatural powers. Therefore, to educate a deaf person or to attempt to give speech to a person for whom spoken language is not "natural" is to go against the gods or to take divine matters into your own hands. Whether truly from the fear of God or simply from the desire to maintain the status quo, such beliefs are the root of indifference and apathy towards underprivileged people in Nepali society.

I have met some deaf women, however, who are determined to break free of this cycle. Because education gives them their greatest resource, which is communication, most live in cities where schooling is available. Given their various conditions, and the variety of personalities I have encountered, I have found the success of deaf women hard to measure. I ask myself, against what standards can they possibly be placed? Because deaf people have been cast out of the social order, is it fair to judge them within it?

I first met Shanti Joshi[12] in a *raksi* (local whiskey) house in one of Kathmandu's oldest market squares. As I entered the dark, one-room parlor on the edge of *Thahity* square, I hit my head on the sunken doorway. Within the confines of its six-foot ceiling and cement floor was the smoke of cheap cigarettes and hot chili peppers. The sounds were Nepali and Tibetan chatter and the whine of rickshaw wheels and tiny motorcycle engines wafting in through the flapping cloth covering the entranceway. As I sat down to join my Tibetan companion for a plate of buffalo *momos* (dumplings), I noticed Shanti, not only because she

was beautiful, but because she was alone. Tucked behind a partially draped veil of her bright orange sari were a dark face and almond eyes. She wore a matching necklace and earrings, her fingernails painted pink; this woman was obviously of high caste. She took a cigarette from her mouth, sipped from her *tongba* and made eye contact willingly. Who was this woman?

It wasn't until I returned a week later and saw her again that I learned that the woman was a regular customer, profoundly deaf, and well known as a prostitute. The proprietor, a talkative Tibetan from eastern Nepal, and a friend of mine, introduced us. I tried some of my Nepali signs with her and, to my amazement, she too responded in formal sign—an indication that she had been educated. However, I had trouble recognizing her name, which she wrote in neat handwriting on an envelope at our table. She then attempted it in a scribbled English which, when combined with a semi-literate bystander's attempt to read her Nepali, became an intelligible name that has never left me.

One of Bhikan Musselman's deaf daughters. Although there is a school for deaf children in her community, her father has chosen to send her to a Muslim girls' school where "at least she can learn to read the scriptures and become a good Muslim wife."

Bhikan Musselman supports his family of ten with his daily wage of forty-five rupees. His children also work as tenant farmers in rented fields nearby to supplement his income with rice.

Over the next three months, Shanti took me to where she slept at night and to the local whiskey and meat parlors where she ate and drank with both urban and rural men. I took her on my motorcycle across town, where she showed me places and faces I could not have imagined existed in the Nepal I knew.

Shanti was born into a sub-caste of astrologers, an ethnic *Newar* family historically indigenous to the Kathmandu valley. Now thirty-six, she was one of the original day-students at the school for deaf children in Kathmandu in the later 1960s and 1970s. Her family brought her up according to the *Newar* traditions, treating her deafness as no exception to

the prescribed route of marriage and children. They eventually arranged her marriage and she had a child. However, whenever I asked Shanti of her husband, her child, her family, her signs always took on a more frantic tone; her face was not angry, but showed a very matter-of-fact defiance. "*No more,*" she once signed with her five fingers cutting across her neck, "*my baby is dead and I've left my husband. . . my family and I don't see each other. They have sent me away.*" It is not clear which came first, her family casting her out or her journey into the world of Kathmandu's prostitution—a way to money and independence.

What is clear is that Shanti has been a prostitute for over fifteen years. When I first asked her if she worked with anyone,

As the rice harvest nears, an aging Muslim widow continues to do her share.

a contented smile came across her face and her pointer finger swooped down into a graceful "one." *"Alone, no one else except for me."* She had a past, she explained: she had worked in India alongside the thousands of Nepali prostitutes that are brought across the border to be sold to brothels. She first became involved in the sex trade when her husband began selling her, working as her pimp, soon after they were married. So why was she in Kathmandu?

Her recollection of life in India brought an animated and memorable story. It was dirty there. Her girlfriends were getting sick, including some of the handful of her deaf prostitute friends. Men would beat her. At this point Shanti's eyes looked suspiciously from side to side, and her painted pointer finger came up to her face, "shhh-ing" over her mouth. After a slight pause, and with the added drama of peering over her shoulder, she slapped one hand under the other and swung it back up again to her chest, beating her pointer finger and palm against the hollow of her sternum. *"I ran away. It was scary for me."*

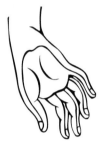

In the beginning of our friendship, because I usually showed up alone, my life brought many questions from Shanti. *"No husband?"* she asked, *"No children? No family here in Nepal?"* With each successive nod of my head, her smile would grow. She would slap me on the back, laugh and then grab both my hands. In sign, she gave me the universal "thumbs up."

Shanti's life is lived day to day. She possesses a spontaneous wisdom that is demonstrated by keen common sense and fearlessness. Taped upon the cement wall of Shanti's one room is a cheap poster of *Laxmi*, the Hindu goddess of prosperity and wealth. On the dirt floor is a tray of vermilion powder and fresh marigolds that Shanti daily mixes with yogurt, rice and water to put an identical *tika* on both her forehead and Laxmi's. Shanti is faithful to a deity of a religion that I wonder how well she understands. She has nothing, but seems to want nothing, save herself. She has found freedom, albeit in an occupation that will not confer her dignity. Even so, her ears do not hear the insults; her beautiful eyes stare down

and defeat the degrading glances of passerby. She is proud.

Although Shanti's courage and independence brought me inspiration, her predicament is precarious. Her landlord, she told me, figures she makes too much money and is raising her rent. She knows little of birth control and continues to endure complications with her health. Two days before I left Kathmandu to return to the United States, I tried to find Shanti to talk to her about AIDS and how to protect herself. The HIV virus is being transported quickly from neighboring India via migrant workers, truckers and traveling prostitutes. I know that just as in America, deaf people in Nepal are left out of the mainstream of awareness and often discover AIDS only after they have contracted the HIV virus. Because she is unable to hear the chattering about this new disease, I wondered if Shanti knew to protect herself. I still wonder, because I never found her again.

When I think of Shanti, I see both the past and the future of her country and her culture. She seems to live both ahead and behind these times in Nepal.

On the one hand, faced with obstacles, she has broken free of her traditional role and is determined to survive on her own terms. She ignores social rules and does not seem to care what people say to and about her, as if purposely turning her ears away from society and the gods and saying "no" to the fatalistic futures that others are too willing to determine for her. I wonder if any other lifestyle within Nepal could grant her the independence she seems to have been born to crave. I wonder if, compared to Nepali women living within the rules of their culture, Shanti is any worse off. With her free spirit at play, perhaps she is even better off.

At the same time, Shanti continues to pray daily to the gods and goddesses of the Hindu faith, emblems of a culture that restrains all she wants to be and all she wants to do with her life. There is so much she will never perceive, so many chances that will pass her by, and so few people who will care. Perhaps the gods and goddesses have given her a spiritual solace in a culture that values neither a deaf person nor a prostitute. She survives. She is proud. I remember

Shanti and think of the many whose deafness has enslaved them. She reminds me how it can also set them free.

For those who do continue to live within the strict confines of Nepali society, a fatalistic understanding of poverty and dependence continues to be a staff bearing the weight of an ancient and complex culture. Fatalism transcends all religious boundaries and traditions in Nepal, whether Hindu, Muslim, or Buddhist, whether a nomad or a poor hills farmer. Even a doctor or government administrator will often fall back on fate as an explanation for the conditions of their lives and their greater community. In their world of so many questions and hardships and few clear-cut answers and solutions, "God's will" is an easy scapegoat. Many Nepalis sincerely feel theirs is the lot they have been given and simply throw their hands up into the air, responding to their experience with the everyday saying "Ke Garne," or "What to do?" In Nepal, to ask the question implies that there is no answer.

Berated by society, maintained by dignity, Shanti Joshi is deaf, with no family and no children. After first being sold by her husband to a brothel in India and surviving in Bombay's red light district for several years, she managed to escape back home to Nepal. She now supports herself working as an independent prostitute in Kathmandu.

*A hidden valley rises to peaks above
22,000 feet surrounding Sringi Himal.*

Hidden Valleys

Tengboche monastery during the full moon festival of Mani Rimdu celebrates the triumph of good over evil. Buddhists from across Nepal come to watch the monks perform the dances of this ancient festival once brought across the Himalaya into the Solu Khumbu region from Tibet.

Sho! Sho! Lha gyalo! Victory to the gods, indeed. I catch my breath and place a stone on the shrine of rock and knotted limbs monumenting the pass and marking the end of an icy four-hour climb. I look north to the mountains of Dolpo, far below to the Bheri River descending from the great plateau of Tibet, and above me to where the clouds faithfully circumnav-igate the Himalayan peaks. My gaze wanders across the ridge towards a series of dots, villages beyond which, my friend and guide Karma Rapkye tells me, we can find a good spot to sleep for the night. It is late in the day.

Just as the sun dissolves behind the mountainside, we approach the village of Jhankot. Crossing the fields of barley, we enter following two farmers, a young man and woman. *"Namaste!,"* my greeting reaches out from behind them. They continue, heads down, balancing the jute straps that hold up a *doko* basket full of loose soil and potatoes. *"Tashi Deleg!"* Karma tries again in his native Tibetan. Still, no response. Too tired to care, we continue on through the village until my

progress is arrested by a short-haired young southerner, looking sporty in his royal blue Adidas track suit and white tennis shoes.

"Namaste, and welcome! Where you are going?" he asks, in an obvious attempt to practice conversational English. I look back to see our last porter trailing well behind us, at least ten minutes back up the ridge. Exhausted, and not in the mood to talk, I undo the belt of my pack, take a seat on the stone wall next to this eager friend, and try to smile. His name is Narayan Banjade. He is the headmaster of the local school, sent from his own village near the Indian border eight days to the south. Karma, who doesn't seem fazed by this turn of events, raises his eyebrows and gives me a smile, then swiftly takes over the conversation and dutifully answers all the routine questions asked of us foreigners.

Their conversation revives me. Within a few minutes I am back in it again, my ears and aching head straining to understand the young man, now speaking very proper Nepali. *"How nice that you have come here by chance! Do you have any medicines?"* he asks me. Ten percent

of the villagers, it turns out, are completely deaf. Most, he says, were apparently born that way. Another local man who eagerly joined our conversation corrects him, *"More like twenty-five percent."* Our silent trailmates from moments ago then walk by and he acknowledges them with the flip of his hand. *"There's two of them. See?"*

We set up camp above the village in the courtyard of Jhankot's two-room school house. The inside floors are the same loose dirt as the ground, the windows merely the absence of stone in the walls encased by short planks of plywood. Within ten minutes of unloading our packs and baskets we are approached by various people from the village. One has heard I am there to meet deaf people, and comes looking for medicine to cure his son's diarrhea. A Tibetan approaches wanting to know if we need to buy any dried yak meat. Another comes to tell us where to retrieve water and offers to take me around to the different houses with deaf people in them.

The people of Jhankot, I learn, practice animistic Hinduism, follow traditional Nepali Hindu cultural codes,

and survive by farming and trading with the neighboring nomads. Living at 10,000 feet in the outer Dolpo region of central Nepal, their home is at the crossroads between the Tibetan mountain culture and that of lower Hindu populations. Although they call themselves Hindu, they also claim to be originally Khampas, having come from the far eastern region of Kham, in Buddhist Tibet, several hundred years ago.

The next morning I visited several families. I first met the "Buddha" family; Mother, Father, four deaf sons, and a new deaf daughter-in-law. They are potato farmers, and when I arrived the brothers went to gather the others so we could talk and I could photograph them together. Quite naturally, they all talked with their hands, albeit in signs I had never seen before, certainly not those known formally as Nepali Sign Language, which I had learned in Kathmandu.

The Buddha family speak their own language. It makes sense to them, and as I started to pick it up it made increasingly more sense to me, too. The signs are specific to their family, the village, and local culture. The sign for "father" is

A sheepherder and his flock take refuge atop the cooling, high hills of the Gorkha region in central Nepal. Once the summer heat has worn off, by late autumn , he will lead them into lower valleys to graze.

the pointer finger on the chin, which corresponds perfectly to the dimpled crease on Mr. Buddha's chin. Many of the signs, such as "food," "to eat," "go" and "come" had a very commonsense, gestured element to them. Their signs are born out of their day-to-day to life in Jhankot, very hand-to-mouth, physically reserved and straightforward.

It is interesting that all the families in Jhankot use this language with deaf people, even those families without deaf members. These villagers live interdependently. They harvest grain and potatoes together every year, they share farmland and the labor of able-bodied sons and daughters during hard times. Even where there is no deaf son or daughter in a fami-

ly, it is probable that people will have worked together with their deaf neighbors at some point and have learned to communicate. Cooperative survival is the rule in this harsh land. Barriers to communication, wherever possible, are removed.

Anthropologists and deaf enthusiasts have studied areas like Jhankot in the United States, the Asian Pacific Rim

80

Two of the Buddha family sons retrieve potatoes from winter storage eight feet below the ground. Their family communicates using a locally-known sign language devised over many generations of deafness in their village.

countries, and South American communities that have unusually high proportions of deaf people. These areas were often found to be home to clusters of genetic deafness and were studied for social and linguistic insights. The researchers have shown that when a high number of deaf people live in a community, the local culture becomes more deaf-friendly and more deaf-centered. Common sense can only support such an observation. As more deaf people live in a community, deafness loses its otherworldliness and becomes more "normal." In the case of deaf families where most family members are deaf, or where the most influential members—usually the parents—are deaf, this is most evident. The language medium, interaction dynamic, and psychological acceptance favor the deaf person.[13]

I cannot say for certain that the deaf people of Jhankot's region are genetically deaf, but I found the remarkable social transformation in both the function and the attitudes of the village that anthropologists find in areas of established pockets of deafness. Unlike so much of Nepal, there was no apparent taboo against deaf men marrying deaf women in Jhankot and, though a deaf member might complicate the life of a family, deaf people did not appear ostracized or unusual. Because I did not find any "deaf-of-deaf" families, where both the parents and their children are deaf, it is not clear that there is a genetic basis. It is certain, however, that some families have deaf members going back several generations.

Another home that I particularly noticed belonged to a small family with a five-year-old deaf daughter. When we arrived, the father walked out of the main cooking room onto the roof of the buffalo stable below. Standing above us, he spoke with the school teacher and then motioned back inside for his child to come outside into his arms. At first, she would not come, and I saw only the smoky silhouette of a tiny figure in a dirty flowered dress. Hesitantly, she walked

The family of Mune Buddha in their mountain village of Jhankot live on their potato harvest and by grazing sheep. Although both parents are hearing, all four of their sons, and their newest daughter-in-law, are deaf.

out into the morning sunlight, her hands partly covering her eyes and face, gazing intently at her father all the time. She wrapped herself around his legs and began to suck on her knuckles. When her father pointed and she saw me, she started to cry. She tried to run back inside, but her father held her firmly, lovingly, and tried to pick her up. *"She's just scared, that's all,"* he reassured me. *"She's never seen a white person like you before."*

It occurred to me to wonder what I must look like to her, in my denim skirt, Hi-Tec walking boots, and with two cameras strapped around my neck. I, too, am "different," just like she is, but she has no tools for interpreting that difference. For all she knew, the same God that made her deaf could have made my skin white. Who was I? Where was I from and why was I here? Like everyone in the village, she was probably curious underneath her fear. But who would, who could, explain the answers to her? How could her father teach her my name and that I was from another country, a faraway place? How could he teach her that there are people, with different names and different faces, living all over a round ball we call the Earth?

Jhankot was different from other villages where I have gone seeking out deaf people. The village seemed more like a single family, like the families I have met who have a majority of deaf members or many deaf children. No one seemed

82   *A deaf woman in Jhankot meets strangers at her door. Startled at first, with the help of sign language (following pages), she realizes she is among friends.*

shocked that I was looking for deaf people or laughed that I even cared. When I told them that I too come from a deaf family, it seemed only natural to them that I could show them some of my own native sign language. I explained the customary basis for American signs like marriage, where two palms are cupped together to signify the holding of hands by sweethearts or in the wedding ceremony. They explained their sign for marriage, which is synonymous with my native American sign "to take," where one hand reaches out as if to snatch something out from the air. Marriage, in this particular village, is an arrangement made in a very straightforward manner by the parents, much like a business transaction. It is an economic exchange from one family to another, where the woman is taken in to a new household as a wife, a cook, and a mother to the new family of her husband. Although such a sign for marriage could appear harsh in a culture flooded with romantic love, in Jhankot it makes perfect sense.

That morning in Jhankot, surrounded by barefoot women, yak sheds, and the increasing warmth of the Himalayan sun, I felt a strange homesickness for a home that I never quite had. All the familiar elements were there for me, but the backdrop was so different. Growing up with deaf parents, I was indifferent to deafness because the life of my parents and their friends was my life. I cannot even say I learned how to live with deafness. I did not. Everything just fell into place as I grew up, and it fell neatly in accordance with my parents' world. I am sure they were much more conscious of their being deaf than I was.

To this day, it seems normal to me, the way we did—and did not do—things. I knew never to shout "*Dad!*" through the hallways of my childhood home or to try calling my mom in the middle of the night from my bedroom down the stairs when I felt frightened, or sick, or needed a glass of water. Without a choice, without thinking really, I conformed to their realities. There was nothing "sad" or "pitiful" to me about our daily life. To get their attention, I would send a vibration their way by stomping my feet on the hardwood floor, flicking a light switch from the other side of the room, or batting at my mother's thighs for her glance when I was knee high. That was normal.

Such conformity to deafness extended beyond our family as well, which only served to further my sphere of what is normal. Where my parents teach, on an American college campus for deaf students, life is centered and prioritized around the deaf majority. There are TTYs (telecommunication devices for telephoning both deaf and hearing people) in every office and at every pay phone on campus. As a courtesy, even unconsciously, hearing people who sign may use sign language with both deaf and hearing people when there are other deaf people around. Accordingly, classes are taught in sign language by both deaf and hearing professors. The Deaf student union plays

music so loud you can feel the rhythm better than you can actually hear it. Unable to call her name, my mother's hearing co-worker used to throw paper clips across the room in order to get her attention. (My mother then, in jest, would throw them right back at her.) Such is the adaptive world of in-betweens for those of us hearing people who live among a deaf community.

Stepping out of that community can be an anxious experience for deaf people. Even though my parents were brought up using spoken English as their first language, in the larger world they are, every single day, like immigrants first setting foot on Ellis Island. Few Americans can "speak" the sign language my parents eventually came to take as their own. When hearing people try to communicate with them, they often scream into their faces with childlike words, as if yelling and gesturing wildly can get an idea across.

So, many Deaf people, whether in the United States or Nepal, have no choice but to live their lives as minorities, with one foot in a hearing world. In the United States, they learn how to write, and in many cases speak and lipread spoken English

(very often "foreign" in both syntax and medium). Many deaf children will sit for endless hours around talkative dinner tables and in front of voiceless television sets with hearing parents and siblings; in their adulthood, they will be expected to apologetically say *I'm sorry, I am deaf, can you please speak slowly* and to carry around a pen and small pad of paper just in case conversations do not work out right. Even though they carry the burden of being different, some deaf people may choose to put both feet in the hearing world anyway, making a choice not unlike that which thousands of foreign immigrants made when they assimilated fully into American culture. They marry hearing spouses, raise hearing children, work as the only deaf person in their office, and socialize and develop their figures of speech and mannerisms originating from the spoken tongue and culture of the hearing world.

The hearing world, *my world*. I was indifferent to deafness most of my early childhood. I was so close to it that I did not ever focus on it. Every day I was a part of our family portrait, and yet I never noticed whether it was black and

white or color. As a deaf family we certainly lived within boundaries, but I accepted those much as I did my mom telling me not to cross the imaginary yellow line marking the end of our playground at the foot of the driveway. If it was childish obedience that told me not to cross into where I could get hurt, I found that the inevitability of growing up stirred a curiosity that threw me directly into the street.

So, as I grew older, deafness became more and more a conscious part of my life as I slowly saw that my family was different, bordering on strange, and most definitely singled out from other families. I began to accept that I would have to take on responsibilities at an earlier age than my friends and that my blissful childhood world had boundaries. People teased me sometimes. Some parents wouldn't let their kids play at my house because "something might happen" and my mother wouldn't be tuned in like other mothers who could hear what was going on. I listened repeatedly to salespersons soliciting donations over the phone replying curtly to me, *"If she's there, then why can't I talk to her. . .*

She's what? ? " Once, at sixteen, just after I had gotten my driver's license, I eagerly begged my mom to allow me to go and pay cash for a check she had accidentally bounced at a plant nursery. Dutifully, she granted me my wish, allowing me to drive across town by myself. I arrived at the nursery and caught the wrath of the store manager. Remembering my deaf mother, he blasted, *"What's wrong, deaf people can't solve their own problems ? "*

That first morning in Jhankot, I considered my state. I am an outsider, a voyeur chasing experience as if I could catch it. I long for somewhere yet I am wary to take citizenship in any one place. I live within contrasting worlds, the Deaf world and the hearing, but also the Nepali and the American.

A growing number of deaf people in the Deaf America in which I grew up are now wholeheartedly cultivating their own identity, their own voice, their own Deaf culture. They are a diverse bunch, varying in ethnicity, race, and the ways they choose to communicate with those around them. Many want to live encompassed by a Deaf world, and thanks to recent laws and social awareness that back their momentum, they are empowered to do that.

In Nepal, meanwhile, most deaf people can barely get their hands out of the dirt, much less learn a standardized sign language that could help establish who they are. Two worlds, both deaf, but born of different resources, different cultures, a different way of being. Within the deaf people of Jhankot, I saw my father, I could envision my mother's expression. I thought of my parents on road trips, in the grocery store, at my elementary school fair. Like those deaf in Jhankot meeting the passerby, my parents carry in them an incredible grace. It is a grace that comes after years of carrying the burden of communicating, of relating, of learning to deal with those who cannot comfortably deal with you.

Although deafness, and to some extent Deaf culture, has been a very large part of my life, as an adult I now try to separate myself from it. As I traveled that mountainside and into Jhankot, I saw only grays: that to define deafness as something that *is* or *is not*, as something that is *good* or *bad*, is to limit and distort the experience. To be deaf means too many different things to different people in different places.

Beyond the sharp definitions of culture and of disability lies infinite space within which we might place ourselves. If we create no boundaries, the possibilities loom endlessly. Therein lies the lucid vision of our beloved and romantic home on the frontier. Our place. Our sense of purpose.

I am a Westerner in the foothills of the *Himalaya*, a hearing person hanging between deaf and hearing worlds. Not quite a stranger, and yet not quite at home in either, I am left dangling inside a foreign land.

Fueled by the recitation of continuous prayer and meditation, porter Passang Lama carries a heavy doko with his ordinary enthusiasm. Passang is becoming profoundly deaf in his advancing age, and works carrying loads into the mountains for at least half of each year.

Nepali children, despite their many chores, share in the universal desire for fun and play.

The Circle of Survival

A deaf mountain man in his late twenties en route from home to the fields. His stunted size suggests severe malnutrition as a child.

It is easy to forgive a deaf child. Even in Nepal, where deafness brings suspicion of greater, evil forces at work, the young deaf child remains innocent, loved and cared for. People are fascinated with the child's seemingly silent world; they play with them; they attend to them—sometimes more than to the other children. But parents soon realize that good treatment, equal food portions and *puja* rituals to the gods rarely give a child back their ability to hear. As the child grows, this reality becomes more and more evident. As fate manifests itself, families of these deaf children become more and more bitter. They begin to mistreat the child, place blame, discount, or take away previous privileges.

Cow dung pressed by hand onto the adobe walls of Nepali homes is recycled into fuel for cooking fires and heating. Once sun-dried, it is a cheap and readily-available energy source, especially in deforested or barren high-altitude regions.

There comes a time when parents stop begging the gods and begin cursing them. As deaf children grow, the barriers of communication begin to multiply, and parents begin to panic. If we send them off with the cattle, what if something happens? How can we call for them? How will this child ever work? What can we teach them, and how? Can the child ever be educated? Married? Even make an income to contribute to the family? For those living delicately on one, or maybe two, harvests per year, planning the year's food consumption demands wise and strategic planning. For nomadic people, which person goes where must be planned in accordance with their ability to work independently, their knowledge of the mountainscape and of the herds.

Parents wonder, how can deaf children fit into these requirements? What about when these children start having children? It is hard enough to feed and find work for the deaf sons and daughters; what if their grandchildren are deaf too?

In Nepal, families cannot afford *not* to consider such questions in their lives. In a land where existence is uncertain, survival is the reward of successful interdependence of man, nature and the gods. Nepalis must compete with the land, each other, and the animals, yet at the same time work together and cooperate with these elements in their lives. To be deaf puts one at a disadvantage in Nepali society because it becomes harder to cooperate and interact with those around you. Tools for survival like effective communication, learning of skills, and social capabilities, do not come easily for the deaf person. As the deaf child's appetite gets bigger and the responsibilities of adulthood loom closer, parents worry whether a young deaf adult will be able to care for them in their old age. Another mouth to feed can often make, or break, a family. In most Nepali households, there is little room for a helpless hand.

In the wealthier urban areas, for those families fortunate enough to live beyond basic requirements of day-to-day survival, a new set of social and caste criteria enter the picture that can further complicate the issues of being deaf. Social pressures are high. When a deaf child is born parents are shamed, shocked and nervous. Families may easily spend more than half their income each month on religious offerings, gifts to priests, and ritual ceremonies that they pray will cure whatever ails their child. As the child grows, in addition to their fears for the child's mere survival, they fear social ostracism.

The questions asked in more affluent countries by parents of deaf children are mostly ideological, as theirs is a world of many choices: Which school will we send our child to? Do we mainstream her, or put her with deaf peers in a deaf school? Is she safe riding the school bus alone this young? Do we use speech or learn sign language for the home?

Nepali families rarely reflect on such things. The question for most parents is not "Which school do we send our son to?" but "Can we send our son to school?

89

Himalayan trading routes, though heavily traveled, are nevertheless dangerous. Balancing across the rockface, this young girl carries water pipes along the four-day trail from Dunai back to her home in Dolpo.

Sonam Yungdrung works as a porter in his native Dolpo region. Like five others in his village, he has become deaf due to what villagers believe is an infected water supply in their community. He will walk for four days carrying twelve-foot water pipes back to his village as part of a new drinking water development scheme.

If we do, who will do his share of chores in the field and home? How will we pay for his uniform and schoolbooks when these things cost one quarter of our monthly income? Is school even worth it? If he studies, will he find a job?"

Families respond in varied ways, depending on their wealth, where they live, possibly their caste, and their faith.

Hari Krishna Dhittal, a twelve-year-old Brahmin boy from a village outside Pokhara, is sent walking alone four hours every day on grassy hill trails, among rice paddies, and eventually to a public bus to get to and from school. In the wintertime, he gets home long after dark. The Thapa family runs a grass hut roadside tea shop in the *Terai* and there are three children ages

eight to fourteen. All three, the daughter and two younger brothers, are deaf. They each attend the government deaf school, a thirty-minute walk. They attend only when they have the time to get away from their work at home. It is Monmaya, the fourteen-year-old daughter, more often than her brothers, who stays behind to help her mother

Two boys routinely carry dried grass along the trail to their village in Dolpo.

wash dishes and prepare tea and food for passers-by and bus passengers. As they live on the border road to India, buyers of young women's bodies have brought generous, and surely tempting, offers to relieve Monmaya's parents of their "burden."

Even those parents who deal most conscientiously with deafness can still fail due to the complexities of social customs and the economy of the local area. Bhikan Musselman is the father of eight children, three of whom are profoundly deaf, one hard-of-hearing, and one, the youngest, now slowly going deaf due to a chronic case of "glue ear." Bhikan is a devout Muslim struggling to get by with his large family in a southern village several miles from the Indian border. His family owns no land, and the only money they have is the 45 rupees per day (90 cents) he earns doing manual labor in a nearby town. Even his eldest son, Jumman, now thirty, deaf since birth and educated in a Nepali government school especially for deaf children, cannot find any paid work. Jumman's wife and their child continually shift back and forth from his and her parents' home because Jumman cannot afford to support them under his father's roof. The four deaf members of the family are the only ones who have learned and now use Nepali Sign Language. Otherwise, they play a hit-and-miss game of speech, gestures, and lipreading.

Even though this family is Muslim, this father nevertheless shares fatalistic

92

beliefs with the local Hindu majority. Bhikan once told me, his tone bitter, his face weathered and defeated:

Two sons and one daughter are deaf. Now what can I say to God? This is God's wish... God made my two sons and daughter deaf. What can I do? These are God's orders, this is God's happiness, what else can I say?

He looks wearily at the future of his children. Not long after that visit, I learned that Bhikan was considering taking his youngest deaf son out of the government deaf school to put him to work in their rented fields. Frustrated and baffled by his eldest son's inability to find any work, even with a better education than many hearing men his age,

he has nearly given up on school and is looking with near desperation towards the days when he and his wife will need care in their old age. *"I am getting old and my son has grown up... Hard times are coming."* Bhikan has chosen not to send his young deaf daughter to the nearby deaf school with her brothers and instead is sending her to a Muslim religious school, hoping to better prepare her to be a good Muslim wife, versed in the scriptures of their faith. The parents of her future husband will be especially concerned about whether she can fulfill a traditional role within the new family, despite her disability.

Making a further effort toward self-sufficiency, son Jumman has undergone training to be a tailor. Sometimes he can

Local men gather in the lower hills of Helambu to help one family thatch their roof, an annual chore.

go to Kathmandu to work in a garment factory. He works sixteen-hour days making $24 a month. Otherwise he stays in his village, harvesting his family's rented land for food wages. I have taken Jumman into the mountains to help me locate deaf people. We have spoken at length about his situation. Of his life back home he told me:

In the mornings I go to [the nearby city] and look all day for work, but it is not available for me. In the evening after I reach home, my mother says to me "There is no food. The bread is finished. The other sons and daughters, nine of them, have all gone to bed hungry."

My own son and daughter are a problem for me because I cannot find work. I can make no profitable income. What can we do about food? Where is our rice?

Jumman and his father bring to mind questions that many are now asking in a rapidly changing Nepal. What use is school to a person and his family if there is no work available afterward? Can a school education put food on the family table today? Gambling with answers, parents

Tikka Ram Dhittal sits outside his family's home in central Nepal and worries about his only son's future. "His ears do not hear, his mouth does not speak. . . Now I am alive so he can eat and he has clothes. But how will he spend his days tomorrow when we are gone? We have no connections with people in high places, so who will give him a job?"

sometimes keep their children at home because they are needed to augment the work force in both the household and the greater community. Parents are told that educated children can be a tool towards a more prosperous life, yet too many families like Jumman's feel they cannot give up the labor capital of a son or, even more so, a daughter for educa-

tion—especially not a deaf child who is seen, a parent once told me, as "an unlikely investment." If parents do send children to school, often they send only one or two, or they pull some out after the primary years. Eldest sons take priority, followed by hearing siblings. Only after that, if free time and money permit, will families consider sending

their deaf children to school. Deaf daughters are usually the last to go.

Sila Dil Kumar lives in the *Terai*, only a few miles from Jumman's house. She is not Muslim, but of the high Hindu *Brahmin* caste, and lives with her mother, an aging widow, and her eldest brother's family. By Nepali standards, they are middle class. They once managed to send Sila to the deaf school for a year. Sila has a mild case of cerebral palsy, which is sometimes found together with deafness. She naturally had trouble keeping up in school because the teachers, overburdened with growing classrooms and lack of training, could not give Sila special attention. Frustrated by her lack of enthusiasm, the family took her out of school after one year and she now lives

A hearing-impaired Tibetan man from the northern borderlands has walked five days south to see a Western-trained doctor. Because he speaks no Nepali, he waits inside a local trekking lodge for someone who can serve as his interpreter.

at home, working effectively as the house servant for this extended family.

I spoke with Sila's mother. Dressed in a thin white sari, she held a certain firm resignation in her face, yet seemed to hang on to some of the fire and frustration that I have seen in many parents of deaf children. Clearly, she worries about the future and considers in the tradition-al Hindu way whether they will ever be able to give Sila's hand in marriage:

What can I say? She's latta, she cannot speak, she doesn't learn any skill and doesn't want to go to school. She learned cutting and sewing for six months, but even now she knows nothing about cutting and sewing. If I die now, she will get so much grief in her life later. She does not have a father, and what if her brother and sister-in-law don't care for her? Well, these things I worry about for her.

She wants to get married... But a clever and smart boy, why would he marry a latta like this?

If somebody else calls her latta, kidding with her, then she gets angry.

96 *Crowds of siblings and cousins pass the time inside a small Muslim village near the Indian border.*

When people see lattos, crippled people, amputees, or those who wear old tattered clothes, then they dominate them, beat them up, throw stones at them and make fun of them. This is a rule here where we live.

It is such "rules" that tie Nepalis to their past and that narrow their visions of the future. Poorer families are further limited by the fact that they cannot afford change. The Kathmandu Association of the Deaf, which is run mostly by volunteer deaf community leaders, estimates that one-half of educated deaf Nepalis cannot find paid work. The deaf young people I have come to know who have found opportunity and developed positive self-esteem often come from the wealthier families with social connections. Not pressed with the worries of day-to-day survival and hard labor, these families can afford to give time to their deaf child and seek out alternatives to the mainstream world that is so often cut off to deaf people. These parents have made a very strong impact on the progress of deaf children.

Sima Thapa talks to her sister, mother and grandmother in a sign langauge developed in their home. Unlike most hearing families of deaf children, her parents and siblings are eager to learn formal Nepali Sign Language.

The family of Sima Thapa is a good example of such progress. Sima is twelve, the eldest, with three hearing sisters. Her father is Jit Bahadur Thapa, a retired officer of the prestigious Nepali Gurkha Army. While his family was stationed in Hong Kong, they discovered that as a newborn Sima had lost her hearing to meningitis. They were advised by the army to return home to Nepal and enroll Sima in one of Nepal's four government schools for deaf children located in the *Terai*. Ten years later, Sima is now the top student in her class and especially enjoys art and drawing. Several of her sisters, as well as Sima's live-in aunt, have learned Nepali Sign Language, and with her parents Sima uses a very developed dialect of "homegrown" signs. Clearly, her deafness has been a challenge taken up boldly by the whole family, and she is treated and spoken to with the same respect and dignity as her hearing sisters.

Sima's mother talked to me at length about her experiences with other deaf families. We both knew her

98   *A rickshaw driver pulls his human-powered bicycle taxi through a monsoon storm.*

understanding and approach to Sima's deafness are not like those of most mothers of Nepal:

Most of Sima's friends, their mothers and their families, do not give them attention. They dominate them and call them bad names and words, like latta *and* latto. *They also make them work very hard, and they don't give*

them food and clothing in the same way they give to the other family members.

The Thapas are an exceptional family, and their acceptance of deafness is becoming contagious. Because Sima became deaf before she ever learned any spoken language, their challenges are of what parents must go through to suc-

cessfully raise a pre-lingual deaf child. However, the Thapas' standard of living has given them the time and leisure to consider options. Poorer families are often unaware that options even exist. Once they do discover them, taking such progressive moves involves change and a price—a risk that not everyone is willing, or able, to pay.

A Gurung sheepherder cuts wool from one of his flock. The wool will clothe his family, be woven into blankets, and possibly sold.

Laxmi Thakali, a deaf tailor originally from the remote Himalayan district of Mustang, has taken risks and is determined to get himself, and his deaf friends, out of a cycle of poverty. He was one of the first deaf students to graduate from a government deaf school in the late 1970s. He now runs a successful shop in the hill city of Pokhara, *Chup Chap* Tailor Shop ("The Silent Tailor Shop"). Laxmi has a presence that is all his own, a little frame topped by a strong and charismatic Tibetan face. His zeal for deaf mountain people takes him back to the land of his parents and grandparents, where he challenges families to give up their deaf children for an opportunity to come and be trained at his shop. He is quick to realize and criticize the low motivation of so many families:

I go to villages and tell parents to send their deaf children to school, but they won't. "We're too poor," they say. But they send their other hearing kids to school. . . This is why the hearing have power and self-reliance and the deaf don't.

High-altitude mountain cultures adjust to
life's exceptional hardships with a seeming
ease and a tremendous grace. In this
Buddhist monastery at 14,000 feet,
a lama passes on both religious and
practical knowledge to young monks.

In the Abode of the Gods

A young mountain girl welcomes a traveling family friend into their village with flowers and offerings of rice. Their families are mith (ritual friends) and stay in each other's homes and share food and drink while traveling.

The life Laxmi Thakali speaks of reflects the many tough challenges for deaf and hearing who live in his native *Himalaya*. The people of the inner and outer Himalayan regions must grapple with their isolation and disconnection from the rest of Nepal. Sometimes, for up to half of the year, the mountain people are locked behind high passes with freezing temperatures. The results of this separation are evident, not just in their different culture and way of life, but in the lack of basic development efforts that are now increasingly apparent throughout the lower regions of Nepal. Clearly the *Himalaya* are the least developed parts of Nepal, with the fewest schools and public water taps.

102   *Sermathang gompa, Helambu.*

Little money trickles in from the government, and foreign aid rarely flows upward into the higher settlements. Although there are obvious logistical difficulties in reaching these people—few roads, sparse and scattered populations, language barriers, and difficult passes—the predominantly Hindu-run Nepali government has shown little motivation to move into these historically Buddhist, low-caste, and culturally alien regions.

Sharing a similar landscape with their kinsmen in the north, for centuries the high-mountain Nepalis living on the south side of the Tibetan border served their own regional Buddhist leaders and later, each successive Dalai Lama, the incarnate spiritual and temporal leader of Tibet. Except for trade, there was little interaction

*Tibetan women of
Saldang, inner Dolpo.*

between the Buddhist dwellers of the high
Himalaya and their southern Hindu neighbors. But in the 1950s this historic relationship with the Tibetans began to suffocate
under the oppressive occupation of Tibet
by the Chinese. While the Tibetan capital
of Lhasa and the more eastern regions of
Tibet were suffering full-force occupation
and the annihilation of their people and
religious culture, the border areas became a
pressure valve and haven for the Tibetan
people. Over forty years of occupation and
resettlement by the Chinese has pushed
many Tibetans over the border into Nepal,
fleeing their homeland via dangerous high-
altitude Himalayan passes. Many have relo-
cated in the Nepali mountains, where they
have become part of the country's voiceless Buddhist minority.

104 *Early morning in the village of Bhi, in the upper Gorkha district.*

Many mountain-dwelling Nepalis still do not speak Nepali and only a small minority are educated in schools. Because the centralized Nepali government has a history of setting up army posts instead of schools in the high Tibetan border regions, the Nepali national tongue is not widespread among the people of these remote enclaves. Buddhist monastic education does remain instrumental in teaching selected youngsters how to read and write in Tibetan, although this is a language few to the south will understand, much less value. It is, however, becoming more possible to send children off to the lowlands for a secular Nepali education. As always, however, when parents can afford such schools, deaf children, along with young girls, are last to go.

A Maatwali Chettri Hindu wears her jeweled dowry of tiger's teeth, Bharuti beads and antique coins. She and her brothers tend their family's herd of seventy goats, grazing them at different altitudes across different regions of western Nepal throughout the year.

Besides the obstacle of financing an education, for the mountain families there are geographical barriers. Families live far away from the mainstream of Nepal, and live far away from one another. Most of the ethnic Tibetan Nepalis live in areas that can be as much as a twelve-day walk from the nearest road head. Some areas that have become popular with foreign trekkers have airports, but flights are irregular and, for most, prohibitively expensive. In the heart of these mountain regions, villages may also be days apart from one another, with only scattered nomad settlements and yaks between. The illnesses—glue ear, typhoid fever—that often cause a child to become deaf are rarely diagnosed in such far away place, and are even harder to

106 *Learned teachers of Buddhism arrive from a monastery in Bhutan to share their knowledge and bring blessings of good fortune to the local Nyingmapa monastic community in the upper Gorkha region.*

treat. For a deafened mountain child, there is no school, few deaf peers, and almost certainly no local educated deaf person to turn to for advice or encouragement.

Yet there is a certain grace. The deaf Nepalis I have found in high-altitude Tibetan-Buddhist settlements are embraced by their families and local culture. I often saw high-mountain people using gestured communication techniques with their deaf neighbors that, even though not a formal sign language, did convey meaning and invite conversation. I found ethnic Tibetans in general to be less inhibited and more charismatic than their countrymen from the south. While they may not have a sign language, they easily become animated when interacting with

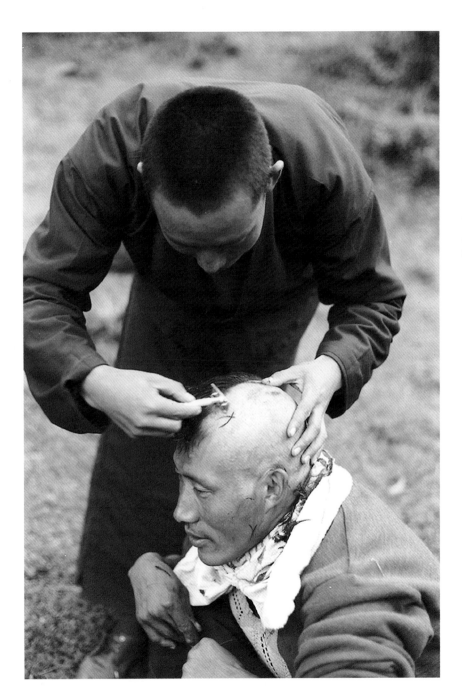

With a razor brought from India, a monk helps out a fellow student with a haircut.

deaf people. The Tibetans seem quick to make up a system of gestures which accommodates the deaf members of their community as well as facilitating interaction for everyone.

Although deaf mountain people are teased, and certainly expected to work hard like their southern counterparts, there appears to be more respect and

Three Ngakpa lay monks, a father and his two sons, inside their portable home. They have traveled far to receive the teachings and blessings of a visiting high priest.

equality granted to them as individuals and members of local society. Based on the deaf mountain natives I met and the conversations I had with ethnic Tibetans, it appears that this difference in attitude is substantially rooted in the fundamental Buddhist belief in the importance of compassion. High mountain-dwelling deaf Nepalis are not treated like outcasts, as they often are in the Hindu communities further south. They are less likely to be hidden and abused or locked behind doors in embarrassment and shame.

Most of the deaf Nepalis I have met in these mountain areas seem to be happier than their rural counterparts further south. One reason may be that

Shanti, a deaf girl from the mountains of Dolpo, meets for the first time a deaf traveler who knows Nepali Sign Language.

they are more included in things. Life in these high-altitude climates is harsh and labor intensive; deaf or hearing, everyone must do their share, and human value can be found in playing a role. I found a gentleness among the mountain people that I did not find as often in the south. I, an outsider, was treated with an unparalleled openness and respect.

I can guess how a family will treat a deaf son or daughter based on how they treat me. Just as respect and consideration were extended to me as an outsider, the community seemed to extend such respect to their own "outsiders," the deaf and otherwise disabled members of their community. Compassion, as Tibetans are taught,

For Shanti and many of the local villagers, Jumman Mussalman is the first educated deaf person, and Muslim, they have ever met.

does not amount to pity or sympathy. Rather, it is an ultimate respect and understanding that life is suffering and everyone—whether deaf, hearing, lowlander, or highlander—seeks happiness and deserves respect in that quest. Following a religion that searches for an inherent good in everyone and everything, these Buddhists are not

only likely to include deaf people with in the circle of humanity, but perhaps even to see them as the invisible teachers of their *dharma*.

Blinded by cataracts and seeking "new eyes," sixty-four year-old Biti Gurung walked four days with the guiding hands of her sister to attend a traveling medical camp. Two days later, after lens-replacement surgery and equipped with an old pair of donated eyeglasses, Biti found the trail back home herself.

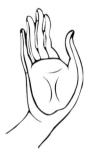

An illiterate deaf farmer from the mountains befriends two educated deaf social workers from Kathmandu. The social workers have come into this remote area to look for deaf people who do not know sign. Although they share no common language with the young farmer, they nevertheless convey meanings with universal gestures and good humor.

Crossing Cultures

Laxmi Thakali, one of Nepal's first high-mountain Buddhists to be educated in one of Nepal's deaf schools, now trains recent deaf graduates in tailoring. After they complete their training, he hires them to work at his successful shop in Pokhara, Chup Chap, "The Silent Tailor."

The interesting and perhaps inevitable trait of the deaf who have made it out of the mountain areas to places where they can learn language and be around a community of deaf people is that they assimilate very quickly into the Hindu mainstream. Like so many Himalayan ethnic groups who have gradually made the exodus south, deaf Nepalis who leave the mountains are quick to leave mountain life behind them. Unfortunately, many mountain people are taught to feel that they are backward, poor and alien to the growing popular culture now connected by transistor radios, roads and the Hindu-izing effects of mountain government posts. Upon arriving in the "new world," some take on common Nepali names (as Laxmi has done), change out of their woolen *chubas* into Western or ready-made Indian clothes, and take on the Nepali national tongue. For deaf people who may not have felt such a strong connection to their mountain culture in the first place, the crossover to this new lifestyle is even easier.

114

Kiran Acharya, coordinator of a nationwide effort to bring Nepali Sign Language to all deaf people and their families, teaches new vocabulary to his enthusiastic new sudent.

When deaf mountain people join the great migration south, they are moving into a land where they will find many more of their own kind. Because the five major deaf schools in Nepal (four run by the government, one private) are all in cities, deaf people often prefer to stay in these urban areas after they graduate. For a deaf person from the mountains who once knew only a handful of other deaf people, and who probably knew no formal language or way of expressing himself, going to the city and finding a deaf community can be a very liberating experience. They take quickly to Nepali urban life, because in many respects, it allows them to become more dynamic human beings and to develop more parts of themselves. Even deaf Buddhists coming down from the mountains and facing the possible ostracism of an urban Hindu society are likely to find a greater emancipation in the growing urban community of deaf people than they did in their villages. Also, being deaf can overshadow the strict social barriers of ethnic identities. Disregarding the conventional Hindu rules of mainstream society, high-caste and low-caste deaf people easily socialize or work together.

Although relocating to the city and settling there into a deaf community may be liberating for deaf people, their families back home are often left in a disillusioning wake. Dawa Lama, a twelve-year-old ethnic Sherpa from the Helambu region, began attending a deaf school two years ago in Pokhara, three days away. Because he had previously studied in the one-room village school with only hearing children, his parents were at first excited when a foreigner offered to sponsor Dawa's education and boarding fees at a school in the city. However, the complications of his departure were soon felt in their lives and in their hearts.

After Dawa's first year away, his parents found they could no longer communicate with him. When they tried to use the sign language they had figured out together as Dawa had grown up, one based on their own local Tibetan culture, Dawa frustratingly corrected them with the "right" way to say things. The sign for his mother was no longer the flat of the hand going from the forehead back to the nape of the neck to signify the sleek, buttered-back hair of traditional Sherpa women, but a finger pointing to the side

The first exposure to sign language Dawa Lama ever got was learning to sign his name. Sign language is often picked up very quickly by deaf youngsters; however, it may take several years to develop a comprehensive vocabulary.

116 *Hostel boarding programs for deaf children give them exposure to sign language on a continuous basis. Om Serchan often casually tutors his students in sign when they are not in school.*

of the nose where the nose ring of the typical Hindu woman would be pierced. The Sherpa language that Dawa could once partially lipread was gradually becoming foreign to him, replaced by the Nepali he was taught at school (the national language is taught in all Nepali schools).

His parents feel frustrated because they are having a hard time learning his new sign language. At the same time, they are struggling with the spoken Nepali that is becoming more and more necessary for trade in their area. Further, because they cannot read or write in either Nepali or their native Tibetan script, and Dawa is being taught only Nepali and some English, the future of their communication does not look encouraging.

Further distancing them, Dawa often stays at school during holidays because his parents cannot afford the time and money to fetch him. Twice, Dawa's long vacation came and went because the letter informing his parents of his holiday time never reached them high in their village in the dead of winter. Not realizing that his parents did not know he could go home, Dawa stayed at his school hostel while most other students from closer villages returned to visit their families. When Dawa does go home, he no longer wants to feast on the rich, buttery and meaty foods of Sherpa culture, preferring the traditional lowland meal of *dal-bhat*.

The changing dynamic between Dawa and his family is not only because he is deaf; many ethnic families whose hearing children go away to school feel a similar estrangement. Eventually, because city life seems to provide a more promising and affluent life for educated young people, many of these rural children forfeit their past in hope for their future.

Dawa's parents feel they are losing their child to the deaf world, but even more to the foreign culture of the lowland peoples. Karmu, Dawa's mother, refers to Kathmandu, other major cities, and even the Hindu villages that are one day (and eight thousand feet) south of their mountain enclave, as "Nepal." The center of her world is mountain country, and all that Karmu knows is her home. Even though her family, like most Sherpas, has lived within Nepal's political borders her whole life, she still feels a strong sense of isolation and otherworldliness in relation to Nepali culture.

Teacher Om Serchan visits the home of one of his school's most promising deaf students. Each day, twelve-year-old Hari Krishna walks four hours to school and back.

117

As boarding students prepare for another day at Pokhara's privately run Srijana School for the Deaf, hostel coordinator Om Serchan quizzes his students on their daily lessons. "I am like a father to them," he says, "we give them so much love, it's good for them."

At the same time, Karmu accepts that only this other world can give Dawa the opportunity his family wants for him. *"What can he do here in the mountains?"* she would say. *"What can we give to him? He has no future here. . ."* In spite of their frustrations, Dawa's parents have shown incredible love and support. Dawa's father and elder brother both mingle with deaf people comfortably when they bring Dawa to the city for school. Like many of the families of successful deaf people I have known both in and out of Nepal, this family has a propensity to adapt and is very accepting of unorthodox ways of doing just about anything. Although Dawa's parents have spoken in tears of the pain and hardship they have undergone to raise their deaf child, their lives are a testament to the many gifts he has given them. They are very flexible and patient, like the Buddhas they honor each morning after waking to the new day. They do not judge Dawa. They love and respect him, not only as their son, but as a vehicle for their further knowledge, worthy of care and compassion.

Teaching a Mind to Talk

"On parents' day this year, only five parents came," *despaired the headmistress of this classroom's deaf school at Lumbini.* "The children often ask me, 'Why don't the bigwigs visit our school like they do the hearing schools? We want to show them our schoolwork too.'"

Schools for deaf children are often where children first come into contact with a significant number of deaf peers. The school becomes the center of their existence, the place where their minds and hands dance in the company of others like themselves. In Nepal, as in many countries, schools become cornerstones of a deaf way of life. In the Nepali deaf schools, students develop idiomatic expressions, innovate signs and expand the vocabulary of Nepali Sign Language. It is here that legacies of deaf people begin and are spread among eager minds, and where deaf children can begin to express themselves and formulate thoughts that they can call their own. Raghav Bir Joshi, a successful

120   *Most of Nepal's deaf children, like this young girl drying her family's clothes upon a school fence, do not get the chance to be educated. Even if there is a deaf school in the local area, deaf children are too often a valuable labor asset and are kept in their homes.*

Kathmandu printer who is deaf, remembers his first experience at a deaf school:

> *When a deaf child goes to school, he begins to meet other deaf kids. Their school is like a central meeting place for kids to come from their isolated homes. They see sign language and start to communicate with each other. Suddenly, their natural language is compatible with someone else's and they become very excited. Deaf people are always attracted to other deaf people.*

The current government school educational policy is to teach "simultaneous communication." Students are taught

Headmaster Surya Mohal and teacher Om Serchan are part of the Deaf staff at the Srijana Deaf School in Pokhara. Their school is the largest and most successful privately run school for deaf children in Nepal, surviving entirely upon donations, foreign sponsors, and a local tuition fee of four dollars per month.

in a combination of Nepali Sign Language and speech. In the early years, much emphasis is placed on speech and oral communication. As students graduate into higher classes, their education takes a vocational slant, often in sewing, carpentry or printing.

To date, only three Nepali deaf students have received their School Leaving Certificate (SLC), which enables them to attend college. This has naturally limited practically all of Nepal's deaf people to traditional vocations and manual work.

Though still limited, the education of deaf children has come very far since the first deaf school opened in Kathmandu in 1968. Originally, the

Hygiene is an important part of the boarding program, as it is often the first time deaf children are taught to care for themselves. At the Pokhara deaf school hostel, fifteen students and two families must share this one water spigot.

schools taught only speech and lipreading and, like many earlier schools for deaf students across the world, deaf students' hands were slapped down if they were caught using sign language or gestures to communicate. According to graduates of Nepal's earliest deaf schools, teachers had little understanding of deafness and, in spite of the introduction into the classroom of a few hand signs which were a cross between British Commonwealth and Indian sign forms, many still did not know sign language. This led to communication breakdowns between teachers and their students. It was often the student who recieved the brunt of the teachers' frustrations.

Fortunately, time and an increased global awareness of deaf people and their education have helped bring progress to

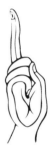

the schools for the deaf children in Nepal. Teachers now have more formal training in Nepali Sign Language, and communication is easier. Students may now go on field trips, attend deaf and disability awareness activities on school time, and are encouraged to interact with local deaf clubs and athletic associations. Further, deaf graduates of the state schools have opened their own private school as well as various training programs across the country. These deaf-inspired programs provide an excellent example for the government schools as well as empowering educated deaf people to share their knowledge with the younger generations.

However, there are still relatively few deaf role models in the school setting. In the four government deaf schools across the country, only one deaf teacher has

124

"If deaf children can come together to study, eat, and sleep, it is very good for their learning," *says a deaf teacher from Pokhara.*

been hired. Most deaf children who begin formal education do so in local village schools, usually as the only deaf student in a large class. Although I have met local teachers who have shown an interest in deaf students, they freely admit that they are generally too overburdened to give that child special attention. Even a hearing child may have a difficult time getting a good education in the standard Nepali school room, where students of different abilities and ages are put together under the tin roof of one large classroom.

Even when families find out about deaf schools, there are other factors that keep the child at home. Besides the financial constraints of tuition, Nepal's few deaf schools are already

"Deaf people are always attracted to other deaf people. . . Schools become a central meeting place for the kids to come from their isolated homes."

overcrowded and limit the number of students admitted. If a child is not admitted in early childhood, or if they have an additional learning disability, their chances of getting into school are further limited. Finally, many families live far from the schools and cannot afford to pay for the child's boarding fees, if boarding is even available.

A further complication of educating deaf children all over the world is explained by Om Serchan, a deaf school graduate and now a head teacher in Nepal's only deaf-run private school:

One of the problems we have is that we teach the deaf kids sign language. In their villages, however,

126

their parents do not understand
their new way of communicating,
and suddenly their ways are
not compatible.

Even though this situation is clearly
developing with Dawa and his ethnic
Sherpa family, this teacher's insight
extends even beyond deaf families.
Because of Nepal's scattered ethnic communities, language barriers alienate even
Nepali families who send their hearing
children away to boarding schools. Like
deaf children learning sign, here they learn
to speak and value the trade languages of
Nepali and English. Over time most lose
articulation in their native language since
distance and travel costs prevent them
from returning home often.

"In their villages, they are destined to a routine life of hard work, cutting grass and portering heavy loads. Such oppression only makes their minds rot and become stale."

The obvious result is a gradual acclimatization to a culture and a language that is not shared by the child's family. The less obvious results are that young people are flocking away from the trades and cultural ways of their parents' generation in an effort to apply their newfound education in the urban centers. Because school does not teach them how to farm, herd animals, and survive in the rural landscape, if they do come back, they find they are actually less "educated" than their peers who stayed behind. This situation applies to both hearing and deaf young people.

The situation for graduating deaf students, however, is more problematic. After being educated and living for years among other deaf young

128 *Many Nepali deaf children, end up as the only deaf students in an all-hearing school. Some are ultimately placed in schools for the mentally retarded where they receive more one-on-one attention from their teachers.*

people, very few want to return to their village, not just for lack of appropriate skills and opportunity, but because they cannot communicate with those back home. Unlike their hearing peers, they have no basic native language skills to fall back on and instead discover their newfound sign to be useless with even their own families, much less their

communities. Today, some parents anticipate rural flight by city-educated children and therefore may purposely keep certain kids at home so as not to lose their help in the village later on.

What happens to the deaf child of a village when they cannot talk to their neighbors? Raghav Bir Joshi reflects further on his rural peers:

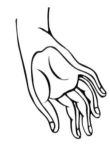

In the villages, in the remote areas, it's not like here in the city, where the houses are one right next to another and deaf people can come together to develop and speak a common language. In the villages, maybe there's just one house here, another one way over there. The deaf child must work in the fields, or just sit in the house all day bored.

They don't learn anything, so their mind just fizzles out. That's how it is in the remote areas. That is the problem.

*Following an increasingly traveled path
for deaf Nepalis, Chandra Prasad Paudel
is employed as a tailor in Pokhara.*

Living Deaf in a Word-of-Mouth Society

With neither formal signing skills nor a school education, forty-four-year-old Birendra Mimali can read and write, has served as president of the local deaf association, and now runs a printing press business out of his house. He attended a public school before Nepal's first deaf school was founded in 1966, but quit in frustration. Says a local villager, "He just copied things out of books until he taught himself to write. . . He's well respected now."

Unlike contemporary Western countries, Nepal is predominantly a pre-literate society built and secured on oral tradition. Less than one-third of the population can read or write, and most of those are children who have recently started school. Culture and history in Nepal are communicated with the present generation not through history books and newspapers, but through the spoken word. With the exception of a written literature passed through the monastic community and religious leadership, the lay people of Nepal learn and share with one another through storytelling. Myths, family legacies, proverbs, and values are passed down in words told while sitting around

132

The Silent Tailor shop in Pokhara is run entirely by deaf Nepalis. Most employees are childhood friends who attended deaf schools together.

cooking fires, while grazing animals, while planting and harvesting crops, or while resting and socializing underneath shaded *pipal* trees.

In a primarily spoken culture, where are deaf people left, particularly when most of the deaf cannot speak or lipread the spoken word around them? Between the lives of deaf and hearing people everywhere, there exists this inherent barrier, but with Nepal's oral culture, it looms even larger. Whether educated or not, with sign or spoken language skills or without them, deaf people of all castes, religions and geographical regions of Nepal feel this barrier. It separates them from their communities, their families, and the subtle resonance of meaning that expresses their cultures.

Defying her family's wishes and social tradition, this deaf woman married her deaf childhood sweetheart. He is Buddhist, and she is Hindu. He taught her how to sew, and together they now run "The Silent Tailor" shop in Pokhara.

Helen Keller, an outspoken and pioneering blind and deaf woman in the United States, once compared her experiences missing each of these senses. "*Blindness cuts people off from things,*" she reflected, "*deafness cuts people off from people.*" Her insight is appropriate to the Nepali people, deaf and hearing, cut off from each other. Few Nepali hearing people know sign language beyond simple gestures, and even fewer deaf people get the opportunity to learn Nepali Sign Language or sometimes any language in schools. Though they live and work side by side, interdependently, they are of two separate worlds, one world based substantially upon the oral tradition they hear, the other upon only what they see.

Raghav Bir Joshi was among the first generation of graduates from Nepal's first school for deaf children in Kathmandu. Raghav grew up as the only deaf member in the household of an influential *Newar* family of the Kathmandu Valley. Now well into his thirties and married with children, he still vividly remembers his younger years

Deaf members of the Gandaki Association of the Deaf pose proudly inside their one-room storefront office. "In 1988, a deaf Italian couple visited our office. They showed us for the first time that there were indeed other deaf people throughout the world, that they belong to their own deaf organizations, and that often deaf people can marry other deaf people. We were shocked!"

and his feelings as an outsider in his own home:

I must honestly say that there were times when I felt more like the family pet than a family member. Because sign language was not fully developed when I was a child, close communication between me and the other family members was lacking. I received food and clothing,

and was sent off to school. I know I was cared for; but I also knew that something was missing in the relationship.

Although very active in the deaf community, Raghav's daily life is spent immersed in the hearing world. During the day he runs a local printing shop with his brother. At night he returns home to his hearing wife

and two hearing children. As is traditional in most Nepali homes, they continue to live in the household of his parents, brothers and their families, all of whom can hear. To communicate with the older members of his family, he speaks, lipreads, and uses some gestures and signs. With his wife, children, and several siblings who have learned Nepali Sign Language recently, he now signs freely.

Suresh K.C. is of a newer generation of urban, educated deaf young men. At sixteen, he has just graduated from the deaf school in Kathmandu and spends his days with his best friends, trading stylish clothes, hanging out drinking sodas at the deaf club, and watching MTV broadcasts from Hong Kong at friends' houses. Although he comes from a strict vegetarian Hindu *Brahmin* family, he is quick to say he has no part in his family's culture. Being deaf, he says, has liberated him from the strict confines of the Hindu way of life.

To look at Suresh, one would think he stepped out of a rock-and-roll music video instead of one of Kathmandu's most ancient family neighborhoods. Clearly, he has found a sense of salvation in the Western pop culture now spreading in the capital city. He plays air guitar all the time, attends Kathmandu's rare rock-and-roll music performances, and walks around town in ankle-high cowboy boots, blue jeans and plaid shirts half-draped over T-shirts depicting reggae and heavy metal music artists.

According to Suresh, there is no room for him in the culture of his family's past.

Obviously, he has given up on a culture that he feels gave up on him and his kind, long ago. Suresh's style, and that of many of his friends living in the increasingly modernized capital city, proposes simple and well-founded questions. Why value a culture that doesn't value you? Why search for yourself in a way of life that grants you no dignity?

He says:

For me, Nepali culture is a mystery. When people talk about culture and follow and teach Nepali customs, they are always talking so fast. How can I know

"If a pregnant woman has too much sex, her child may become deaf," *goes a traditional saying in this village in the Mustang district. Undaunted by local superstitions, Dilmati Serchan and her deaf daughter, Shanti, laugh in spite of such beliefs.*

A Muslim mother, her deaf daughter, and an aunt outside their home in the southern Terai. Says the young girl's father, "I will not send my daughter to the deaf school, what job will that give her? I will send her to the nearby Muslim school for girls. At least there she can learn to become a good wife."

what they are meaning when I've never heard the words, the songs, and the voice of that culture?

For so many generations, from my great-grandparents to my father and finally down to me, we have been Brahmins. They always wanted me to study the scriptures, do puja (ritual ceremony), so they would lead me around by the hand through something I have never been able to understand. My head would spin at this hearing culture and I was made to feel so stupid all the time.

So I have since put Brahmin and hearing culture aside. I've given up on all that. A speaking culture is no good for me. Instead, I've looked outside to foreign cultures and to their way of doing things,

Celebrating Losar, the Tibetan New Year, a deaf elder joins the ritual festivities with the help of a hearing aid, an uncommon, and expensive, device among Nepal's deaf population.

and I like how they seem to be so free. There's no such thing as Brahmins because everyone is the same, like one group.

Now I've put on a new uniform that is my own culture. I feel a lot more free this way. If I want to eat meat, or do whatever, then I am free to do so, because what's the meaning of all that anyway?

With the first generation of deaf school graduates reaching middle age, and a recently formalized Nepali Sign Language now spreading across the country, early signs of a deaf culture are forming. Not all the members have a perspective as proud and defiant as Suresh's, nor as successfully integrated as Raghav's, yet most educated deaf people are very aware, and increasingly proud, of their identity as deaf people. Spurred by what they hear about flourishing deaf cultures in America and European countries, the relatively small but growing educated deaf population of Nepal is recognizing that deaf lives consist of unique elements bound by a common language, Nepali Sign Language. More and more, they are articulating a Nepali Deaf identity.

*Young deaf professionals from
Kathmandu spend a festive afternoon
playing cards at a holiday picnic.*

Cultural Cowboys

Deaf men are more likely than their female peers to enjoy freedom after finishing school. Many choose to stay in the city, find a job and live on their own. Leaving their families and the financial support they grant is a difficult and risky step, yet more and more are taking it. Many deaf people who stay in the cities find a new family in the deaf community there.

In the early 1980s, the first association composed mainly of deaf people was founded in Kathmandu. It took a decade for the government to recognize the Kathmandu Association of the Deaf. Since they have become an official non-government organization, however, their successes have solidified. KAD has assisted other, smaller cities to form their own deaf associations. Local and government support continues to be meager, but with the help of foreign financial assistance, especially from deaf and disabled organizations in Western countries, there are now approximately ten similar deaf organizations in Nepal.

A local deaf association is of great help to deaf people, their families, and the process of strengthening a deaf community. Families can find educational options for their deaf children; deaf young people can meet and socialize with others; and, in the larger offices, local people have the opportunity to both learn and teach Nepali Sign Language.

The officers of these associations are deaf themselves and sensitive to the needs and issues that concern deaf people in Nepal. Although they have little

"Sign language is very important for deaf people because it is our own language."

administrative experience, some have nevertheless managed to set up programs and projects including vocational training programs for uneducated or partially educated young deaf women, cooperative work on documentary television programs with foreign producers and local aid offices, athletic federations, social events, picnics, and annual leadership elections.

This young and energetic leadership has been the cornerstone for building an expanded deaf community in Nepal. Deaf people are starting to find their own way, and the deaf leaders are now becoming stewards of a developing Nepali Deaf history. Nirmal Kumar Devkota is a past president of the Kathmandu Association of the Deaf. He was also one of the first deaf students to study in the country's

"When deaf young people see me speaking and signing, it has a great effect on them," says Nirmal Devkota, the first and only deaf teacher in Nepal's government-sponsored deaf school system. "I am deaf just like they are. And so I become a good role model for them."

first deaf school just twenty-five years ago and is now the first deaf teacher to teach in that school. He reflects on the progress that has been made so far:

Before it used to be that hearing people would stand in front of deaf people in order to help them. Deaf people were always in the background and could never actually see what was going on; they were in the dark.

Now, that has all changed. There are two paths: one is the Deaf road, and the other is the Hearing. A hearing person might give assistance to people on both roads, but is always likely to pay more attention to his own road, which is the way of the hearing people. If any hearing friend were to ask a favor, he would turn to the deaf people and say "Just hold on. I'll help you tomorrow, maybe the day after." Well, deaf people can end up waiting their whole lives, jobless and idle.

These days it is different for us. Deaf people are in the forefront of their own lives and the hearing people are in the background. Because they are compatible with other deaf people, they are one and the same and are more likely to help one another out. The hearing people have

Banners of signing hands are marched through the streets of Nepal's capital, Kathmandu, on the United Nation's proclaimed "World Day for the Disabled." Each year draws approximately 200 deaf, blind, and otherwise disabled people to the streets in a proud display of their identity.

their own way, and they help their own too. So each group helps themselves, and this ultimately will make the Deaf a stronger people.

Laxmi Thakali, from the high-mountain culture of Mustang, and founder of the Silent Tailor Shop in Pokhara, has a similar determination. For years he effectively ran his own school, teaching young men how to sew and how to stand up for themselves. His shop is a shanty made out of tin, wood planks and cardboard, its walls postered with the handbills of deaf conventions and gatherings that friends have sent him from different parts of the world.

When Laxmi first set up shop, his strategy was to charge 5 *rupees* (10 cents) less than the going rate for sewing clothes.

That way, he says, people in the community would give him a chance. Now, his business is thriving and he has a sophisticated working staff of five, all deaf. In a society that bargains for everything, I asked Laxmi how he communicates with the local hearing people.

A regular customer approaching the shop gave him the chance to answer me.

142 *Sisters, cousins and aunts gather around deaf bride Shrijana Shrestha at a wedding party in her parents' home. Following an increasingly popular trend, Shrijana has been allowed by her parents to marry her childhood sweetheart, who is also deaf.*

Laxmi grabbed a stick from just inside the doorwell and, with his customer, went outside where he began to draw lines in the sand. Although I could not make out the Nepali script they were writing, I could tell by their faces that they were busy negotiating. In a matter of a few seconds, they both smiled and Laxmi returned inside to get

the newly tailored slacks in exchange for seventy *rupees*.

The opportunity that Laxmi has created for himself and given to young deaf people is relatively rare, but inspiring for others. Although originally a Buddhist, he has since married a deaf Hindu wife, whom he met at his deaf school. Together they have one hearing son and

are quite famous for their unique business venture and charismatic rapport with the locals. In his fast-moving poetic sign, Laxmi once told me:

Deaf people have to stick together and work hard to make themselves strong. Hearing people have their way of doing things, and we have our own as well. Hearing people have so much more than we do, their position in society is so much higher. We have to struggle to make ourselves more equal with them. We have to work hard at our jobs and discover that we have our own way of doing business, just as the hearing have their own way of doing theirs. The government has to give us opportunities too; they have to give the help they give to the hearing people to the deaf people too. Deaf people need to be given a chance.

And more and more deaf people finally are being given those chances to prove themselves. Jagadish Dawadi is one of the first deaf Nepalis to get his School Leaving Certificate, making him eligible for higher education. To prepare for the SLC, he had to continue his education at a hearing school until he was eighteen.

I studied in school, but it was hard. The teachers only spoke and I could not hear them, so I would just keep quiet and studied my books. I concentrated on learning everything from my school books and then later discussing them with my teachers. I never profited from all their talk in the classroom.

I've heard that in America there are deaf universities. When I found out that there are entire universities for only deaf students, I was shocked, I couldn't believe it! So I thought, "That's what I need to do, that's where I would like to go."

It did not take long for Jagadish to get hold of applications to American colleges with deaf support programs. Currently, Jagadish is studying social work at the National Technical Institute for the Deaf, an all-deaf college in Rochester, New York, on a full scholarship from the Institute.

Another source of empowerment among deaf people that is becoming more and more common even within higher caste families is the marriage of deaf men and women. Traditionally, parents have been wary of marrying their deaf children to others who are also deaf; many parents never even bother to arrange a marriage

Shrijana Shrestha sits obediently in the viewing room of her parents' home, where family and friends come to greet her. In the tradition of her Newar caste, she wears a red sequined veil which will be removed once the priest has completed the wedding rituals.

143

for their deaf child, considering that fate has doomed them for life. The perception that a deaf family member will be a financial burden for families is another reason parents rarely choose such a union for their deaf son or daughter. I have been told, *"One deaf child is hard enough, how could I possible choose to bring in another?"* This concern covers not only logistical and financial difficulties, but social stigmas as well; high-caste families especially are inclined to marry off their deaf son or daughter to a hearing spouse in hopes that this will compensate for the deaf person, making them more normal and accepted in the family. Sadly, I have seen such marriages end in separation, though the separation can be an empowering rite of passage for the deaf spouse.

The mother of Kalpana Shrestha of Kathmandu prepares her deaf daughter to meet her new husband and the Buddhist priest who will marry them. Kalpana's husband is also deaf and fortunately, of her same caste. "We want her to be happy," says Kalpana's father, who also has a deaf son in the family.

Whatever the real value of these worries may be, some elders overcome them. The Shakya family is an excellent example. Devendra and Pramela are both deaf and now married, even though they originally come from two different castes which, by religious and social standards, provided grounds for incompatibility. Against their parents' wishes they went ahead and married. After a very difficult adjustment period of several years, both are now fully integrated and accepted back into his family's household. Following tradition, Pramela moved into her husband's house along with his family and has taken on his profession. As a team, they are artisans, handcrafters of silver and metal picture frames and religious statues. Their business is successful and has allowed them to employ three other deaf metal smiths.

Pramela's husband, Devendra, remembers his own family's concerns when the time came for him to marry:

Deaf or hearing? My family asked me which I wanted to marry when I was younger. "I want a deaf girl," I told them, "because deaf people together make us

The hands of deaf bride Kalpana Shrestha are adorned in traditional gold jewelry and painted ornately with henna.

stronger." Hearing people always shy away from deaf people, "A deaf wife would be better," I told them.

"But what about your children?" My family worried. "Will they be able to hear? How will you communicate with them?"

Pramela uses her own experience to build a passionate platform to help other deaf women:

When we were first to be married, our friends were so excited. The first deaf man and woman to actually elope! Before it used to be that families with a deaf son would always marry him to a hearing girl, leaving no one for the deaf girls to marry. In Nepal, there are so many problems for young deaf girls. What to do with them? Parents say, can we still marry them?

What will they do? Can deaf people marry deaf people? If they can find work together, maybe the parents will consent. But what if the deaf husband and wife can't? This is what so many parents fear.

And then, when the deaf daughter goes to the new husband's house, will that family love her? Will they give her attention or be mean to her and discriminate against her?

Undaunted by the caste rules prohibiting their intermarriage and their parents' fears of bringing more deafness into the family, Pramela and Devendra Shakya eloped. "At first it was very difficult," Pramela recalls, but eventually they were both welcomed in the traditional way into Devendra's extended-family's home. They now run a successful handicraft business and raise their two hearing children, both of whom are fluent in sign.

Pramela's worries are not just for the fate of young women in Nepal. As more and more deaf people marry and become part of the extended family of the mother culture, such questions will be in the minds of all deaf people. Many wonder what will become of their futures, their opportunities both within and outside of their local communities. Will they be accepted in their new roles in society? In a society competing sometimes desperately for survival, can deaf people be respected as building blocks or must they be used only as the beasts of burden?

Pramela and Devendra have since had two children who are both hearing. Ages seven and nine, they are growing up in a tri-lingual household that speaks Nepali and their ethnic Newari language, as well as Nepali Sign Language. The younger family members are even becoming adept at a fourth language, spoken English. Contrary to his parents' fears, Devendra's children and family have adapted naturally to deafness in their home.

When I think of the future, I see much change that will benefit the deaf people of Nepal. Adapting to the heavy influx of Western culture and development has created a new range of problems for the Nepali people. The secularity of Western thought, however, is clearly benefiting those deaf people who were once cast out of a strict religious moral code. Across the country, Nepalis are beginning to open their eyes to the deaf people in their families and communities and to see them in a new light. Hearing people are making efforts to learn Nepali Sign Language, and an increasing number of deaf children are being taught this language from their earliest years at deaf schools.

From an international perspective, deaf people are being recognized as another tribe in the global village. Deaf cultures are being appreciated as an interesting lens for viewing larger cultures surrounding them. The signs and value systems of a deaf culture are woven tightly into the mother society and the history of her people, yet provide a different perspective. To understand something about the lives set forth in these pages is to understand something about Nepal. By knowing her deaf people, it is possible to glimpse the world that has enveloped and developed them for centuries.

148 *Larkyl Lama, a Sherpa Buddhist from Helambu, ponders the future of his deaf son, Dawa. "Im not sure what I can do for him, but whatever I can, I'll try."*

Like a journey on many of Nepal's back roads on which I have traveled to find these people, the lives of deaf Nepalis are rough and unpredictable, seemingly unfair, riddled with hypocrisy and mercilessly tied to an antiquated past. Yet I am reminded that a way is made only by walking these roads. These deaf people's voices, their dancing hands,

can be heard with the courageous heart. Their lives are testament to the diversity of the gods and goddesses that appear to curse them. They embody Nepal, yet they tear away from it. Resonating between these options of participation and rejection lies a pilgrim's path to the mountainside, the templescape, and the internal landscape of Nepal's people.

In a time when the world is heading towards homogenization and conformity, it is reassuring to see deaf people articulating how they are different. They are creating new communities in which the visual symphony of their culture can thrive. Deaf Nepalis are discovering their voices. They are ready for the rest of the world to open their eyes and ears and recognize them.

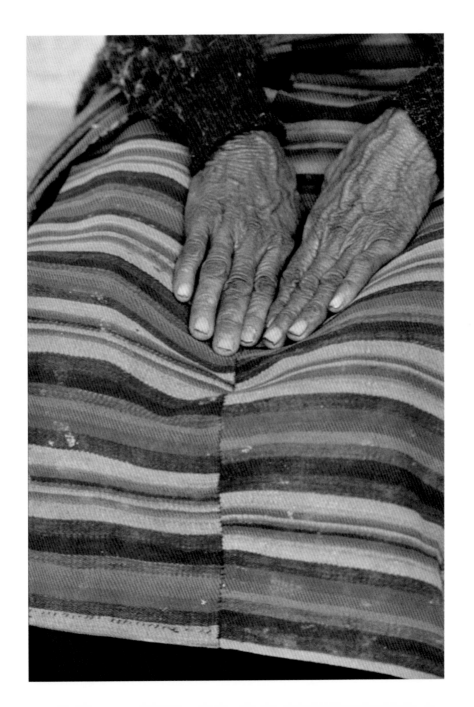

Notes

1 Sogyal Rinpoche (1992).
The Tibetan Book of Living and Dying.
First published Harper Collins
Publishers, Inc.,
San Francisco, 1992.
Quote taken from Rupa and Company
edition, New Delhi, 1993. Page 200.

2 Pre-lingual deaf people are those who
become profoundly deaf before they
learn spoken language. This would
account for all children born deaf as
well as most of those who lose their
hearing within two to three years
of age.

3 American and French sign languages
enjoyed a period of accepted use in
schools of the 19th century, but then
came to be shunned in favor of speaking and lipreading spoken language.

4 Broughton Coburn (1991). Nepali Aama:
Portrait of a Nepalese Hill Woman.
Chico (CA): Moon Publications.

5 Dr. Mana Vajracharya. Interview,
Kathmandu, May 25, 1993.

6 Sogyal Rinpoche (1992).
The Tibetan Book of Living and Dying.
First published Harper Collins
Publishers, Inc., San Francisco, 1992.
Quote taken from Rupa and Company
edition, New Delhi, 1993. Page 92.

7 Ibid. Page 93.

8 Ibid. Page 97.

9 Dor Bahadur Bista (1980). Fatalism
and Development: Nepal's Struggle
for Modernization. Hyderabrad:
Orient Longman Limited. Page 77

10 Ibid. Page 81.

11 Ibid. Page 79.

12 Name has been changed.

13 Woodward, James. Seminar at 2nd
Annual Asia-Pacific Conference on
Deafness, August 1992. Pattaya,
Thailand.